I0438254

Timeless Writings 16

Collection of Articles

Tatay Jobo Elizes, Pub.
July 2014

-ooOOoo-

Self-Publisher/Compiler/Printer

Tatay Jobo Elizes, born 1934 in Manila, now senior ctizen in Brooklyn, NY. Besides self-publishing, he is busy in piglets dispersal programs for livelihood projects in the Philippines via internet.

Acknowledgement

Gratitude and acknowledgment belongs to all contributing writers who gave their permission to compile all articles in a book like this to record history based on timely events that directly or indirectly affect our lives. Copyrights of each article belong to the particular author and he/she is free to re-publish anywhere, without any restriction.

Dedication

I dedicate this book to **all Filipinos** all over the world and to my immediate family, friends and relatives.

This book has the following ISBN numbers:

ISBN-13-978 - 1500688509   &   ISBN-10 - 1500688509

Disclaimer:

Views are expressed by the authors alone. Tatay Jobo Elizes does not knowingly publish false information or commit copyright infringement having been given explicit permission to publish this book. Tatay Jobo Elizes may not be held liable for the views of the author exercising his/her right to free expression.

Contents

Introduction

Writings are timeless as they act as mirrors of history. Let me explain why I publish writings. You don't have to be a good writer to write something. The only requirement is to write in simple terms to be understood. I have seen a lot of good writings in the internet, in magazines and newspapers. But most writers have only one or two articles and therefore not enough material to be published as a book. And yet, many of them need to be published. So the idea of collecting all these various writings hit me. I myself cannot come up with enough material. I decided to offer my services to publish anybody's worthwhile writings in one fairly good sized book, in paperback or pocketbook form. Their ability to publish is solved in a nutshell.

I am offering these services free of charge because of the availability of print-books-on-demand (POD) system nowadays. I have acquired the knowledge the hard way. I am now in a position to help publish writings of anybody. I can produce the book, but it's not entirely free of cost on my part. I merely assume the cost.

Why put your writings in a book? And not just in the internet? I recommend that writings be retained in a hard copy or in book form or printed form for posterity. The book will always be there among your collections or libraries. Not all use the internet. The internet access has its technical problems. Writings in the internet may be erased erroneously. Free storage is hard to access. Paid storage may be returned or lost.

For those looking for a publisher, especially if you have a novel or many essays, I can produce the paperback book under your own authorship. Book sale is risky business. In most cases, I cannot even recover my initial costs. As authors, you must help in marketing these books that contain your writings.

1

The Martyrs of Camarines Norte

A Narrative Account of the Katipunan in Camarines Norte *and the Daet Revolt of 1898 + Researched and Prepared* **By Mr. Roland Bayhon, Natonal Historical Institute, Atty. Vivencio F. Abano, Mr. Gregorio Pimentel Jarencio and Descendants ol the Martyr Jose Abano** Dateline: July 1992, Camarines Norte

Preface to this Article

The school children of Camarines Norte study and learn from their history class about the patriotism and heroism of **Jose Rizal, Andres Bonifacio, Emilio Aguinaldo, Antonio Luna, Gregorio Del Pilar,** sons all of Laguna, Manila, Cavite, Bulacan, llocos and the provinces. But not of Camarines Norte.

Unfortunately, our school children and even most of our province mates do not know nor have heard about Camarines Norte's very own sons who were no less heroes and martyrs of the Revolution. They would certainly take greater pride in their roots and the province of their birth if only they knew.

This account tells about the beginnings of the revolutionary movement in Camarines Norte, the Daet Revolt in 1896 and the men who participated in that uprising against the Spaniards.

It is by no means a complete account. There is still so much to be done so that the heroism and sacrifices of the Martyrs of Camarines Norte may be fully known, recognized and appreciated.

While many of the Martyrs have been identified many more still remain unknown. And even of the named ones, certain questions yearn for answers. Who were they in the community of their time? What were their ideals, then values, their beliefs and principles? What exactly was their participation in the Revolt? When, where and how were they tortured and/or killed?

It is hoped that in the near future these questions will have answers and that all who suffered aand died in the Daet Revolt will be known and thereby be a cause for pride and honor among the people of the province.

Martyrs' Chapter 1: The First Katipunan in Bicol

Carnarines Norte has the enviable distinction of being die first province in the Bicol region to organize a Katipunan and to give direct assistance to the Philippine revolutionary movement.

Prior to the outbreak of the revolution in 1896, there existed in Camarines Norte certain cooperatives. Agricultual producers supplied these cooperatives with abaca, copra and other products, which were then sold by the cooperatives without passing through middlemen. Part of the profits of the cooperatives was secretly remitted to the revolutionary movement of Andres Bonifacio.

The cooperatives also served as effective through covert means of spreading the ideals of the revolution. Their members could move around freely without arousing the suspicion of the Spanish authorities. While outwardly buying the produce of (he farmers in the different barrios and towns of Camarines Norte, they were also able to inform those who were receptive about the activities of the then Manila-based revolutionary movement. In this manner, many Filipinos in the province became aware and sympathetic to the cause of the Katipunan. These included not only the intellectuals and educated class, but also the farmers and laborers.

The formalation of the cooperatives was promoted by the *La Cooperativa Popular*, founded sometime in 1894 by **Don Vicente Lukban y Rilles**. a former Justice of the Peace of Labo, Camarines Norte. Lukban was born in that town m 1860, but both his parents were from Tavabas/l/.

Lukban was arrested by the Spanish authorities in 1896 because of his political activities, and was incarcerated in Manila until August 1997. Upon his release, he immediately joined General Emilo Aguinaldo and was commissioned to serve as one of his staff to the armed forces of the revolutionary government.

/1/ New Quezon province

On orders of Aguinaldo, Lukban extended the insurrection to the Bicol region. In November 1897, he carried out secret communications with **Don Alfonso Moreno/2/,** a prominent resident of Daet. The communications were coursed through certain Filipino officers of the merchant ship, *Taal,* who were partisans of the revolution. Lukban entrusted to Moreno the organization of a Katipunan unit in Camarines Norte, and advised him to await arms and further instructions from Aguinaldo's headquarters in Biak-na-Bato.

Moreno started the organization of the Katipunan that very same month of November 1897. He did not encounter any difficulty since many Filipinos in the province were already sympathetic to the cause of the Revolution. Membership swelled rapidly due in great part to the ground works prepared years earlier by the cooperatives. The Katipunan in Camarines Norte attracted many followers and sympathizers, including not only prominent Filipinos of Daet and the other towns of **Labo, Talisay and Calasgasan/3/,** but also the *principalia/4/* and employees of the courts. Even the fifteen native soldiers of the local detachment of the *Guardia Civil* became partisans of the Katipunan and are receiving secret instructions from Moreno.

Moreno was the head of the Katipunan m Camarines Norte. His leaders or lieutenants in the organization were **Telesforo Zaldua**, *teniente mayor/5/,* **Jose Abano**, *capitan mumtcipal/6/* of Daet, **Domingo**

Lozada, former *capitan municipal,* **Gavino Saavedra**, and others.

/2/ *Moreno Street in Dart is named after him. .*

/3/ *Calasgasan was a municipality at that time, and became a barrio of Daet during the American rule.*

/4/ *important residents/members of the community.*

/5/ *Chief Lieutenant second to the capitan municipal or gobernadorcillo in the government of a town.*

/6/ *The gobernadorcillo, or head of a town similar in some ways to the present-day mayor.*

Martyrs' Chapter II: The Month of March 1898

Unrest began to be felt in the Bicol Region.

Rumors circulated in Daet about a disturbance that would take place on the feast day of the *Anunciacion* when members of Spanish community, including the parish priest of Daet, **Fray Juan Perdiguero/7/** would be killed. Nothing happened on that feast day, nor on the following day when it was said that the rumored plot would definitely take place.

Yet, the rumors persisted The Spanish civil and military authorities decided to investigate. The head of the local *Guardia Civil,* **Lieutenant Maximiano Correa,** called those who were suspected or accused of being members of the katipunan. They denied the existence of the Katipunan in Daet or in any part ot Cajnarnses Norte. Lt. Correa was satisfied and let them go.

However, the Spanish community of Daet continued to suspect that some plot against them was afoot. They took the precaution preparing the house of **Florencio Arana,** a Spanish merchant of long residence in Daet, as their refuge and defense in case of any disturbance or uprising/8/.

Martyrs' Chapter III: The 13th Day of April 1898

The Pact of Biak-na-Bato was signed by General Emilio Aguinaldo and the Spanish government. Aguinaldo lrft for exile in Hongkong. One of the members of his entourage was Vicente Lukban.

/7/ The friars in Bicol region were front the Franciscan Order.

/8/ Evidence indicate that the house of Arana was near the northwestern corner of the present Vicente Basit Street and Justo Lukban Street, a short distance from the old Spanish bridge then named San Narciso Bridge.

Moreno felt that the Katipunan movement in Camarines Norte had to rely on his judgment and on their available resources In the absence of Lukban. With this in mind, he continued to make preparations to strike against the Spanish authorities in the province.

In April 1898, Moreno issued a call from the barrio of *Barra/9/* to the members of the Katipunan and gathered them in the barrio of Mampili.

Since the Katipuneros were without firearms, except for the fifteen native members of the *Civil Guards*, Moreno's plan to take the Spaniards by surprise.

Unfortunately, in the late afternoon of April 13, the scouts he had sent ahead to Daet committed the mistake of appearing and displaying their bolos and red pennants at the Daet *market/10/.* Someone shouted *"Insurrectos!"*, causing the people in the market to panic and run.

The Spaniards learned of what had happened. That very same evening, they gathered their families and transferred to the house of Arana. They took refuge there and prepared to defend themselves. To deprive any attackers of cover, they took the precaution of demolishing the nearby Chinese houses and stores.

That same evening, two Filipinos were apprehended by the Spaniards on suspicion of being Katipuneros, and were put in jail.

Meantime, the Katipuneros who were already at the outskirts of Daet decided to go to the barrio of Barra. Before doing so, they cut the telegraph lines to Nueva Caceres so that the Spaniards could not ask for help or succor from there. Most of the Filipino inhabitants of Daet also left in fear of an anticipated battle between the Spaniards and the Katipuneros.

/9/ Barra became the municipality of Mercedes m 1948.

/10/ *The market at the time was near the church and the present site of the CANORECO office.*

Martyrs' Chapter IV: Events of the 14th Day of April

Lt. Correa called for the *capitan municipal* of Daet. **Jose Abano,** and asked him about the events of the previous night. Abano pretended not to have any knowledge of what had happened, and denied reported sighting of the katipuneros.

Upon insistence of the Spaniards, **Lt. Corrca** left the house of Arana with eight Civil guards and a Spaniard named **Domingo Chacarretegui** to go to Barra. On their way, they encountered the Katipuneros, who attacked them. The party of Lt. Correa withdrew and, whil retreating towards the direction of Daet, fired at the Katipuneros pursuing them. The native civil guards, however, were aiming above the heads of Katipuneros. This was observed by Lt. Correa and Chacarrategui and made them suspect the loyalty of the native civil guards.

When they were running short of ammunitions, Lt. Correa ordered one of the civil guards to run ahead and get more ammunition from Daet. The corporal of the Civil Guards who had remained in Daet was a native. He refused to give the ammunitions in the absence of a written order from Lt. Correa. It was Arana who grabbed the ammunitions from the corporal and brought them to Lt. Correa. The actuation of the corporal heightened the suspicion of Lt. Correa and the other Spaniards about the native civil guards.

It was already 9:00 in the morning when the party of Lt. Correa managed to get back to Daet and the safety of the house of Arana

The Spaniard! moved in food supplies and medicine in anticipation of prolonged siege by the Katipuneros. They also succeeded in repairing the destroyed telegraph lines, and were able send messages to Nueva Caceres ahout what was happening in Daet.

That same day, the friars from the neighboring towns of Daet arrived at the house of Arana. The last to arrive in the afternoon were **Fray Antonio Mirablanca,** the parish priest of Basud, and his brother **Siro Mirablanca.**

The house of Arana had then been converted into a fortress. Defending it were twelve Spanish military men, the functionaries of Daet, and some businessmen and employees. There were also the fifteen native civil guards who were In secret league with Moreno All In all, the defenders consisted of about fifty persons armed with rifles.

Martyrs' Chapter V: Events of the 15th Day of April

The Spaniards arrested **Telesforo Zaldua.** They had already learned that he was one of the leaders of the Katipunan. He was ordered tied and placed under guard together with two other Filipinos imprisoned earlier in the evening of April 13. His brother, **Marianito Zaldua**, was also arrested.

That same day, the Judge of the Court of First Instance accompanied by two other Spaniards and two civil guards went to the house of the Zalduas. They interrogated **Tomas Zaldua,** father of Telesforo and Marianito and a former *capitan municipal* of Daet. They ransacked the house to find evidence about the Katipunan. Not finding any, they took with them two trunks of documents and belongings for further scrutiny.

Nothing else happened that day until about 4:00 in the afternoon when the Katipuneros launched their attack against the Spaniards, who had taken refuge in the house of Arana. The Spaniards were ready and greeted the rushing rebels with a volley of fire. Three from the attackers coming from the old Spanish bridge were hit in the first discharge.

The Katipuneros then tried to flush out the Spaniards by setting fire to the house of Arana. But the Spaniards had made ready a hundred wet sacks and used them to extinguish the blaze.

In uncontrolled rage, Lt. Correa shot all the bound Filipinos who had been arrested earlier by the Spaniards. Some of the Friars, particularly the parish priest of Daet, fray **Perdiguero,** tried but failed to stop him. Among the prisoners killed were the brothers **Telesforo and Marianito Zaldua.** The fighting lasted for six hours until 10:00 in the evening.

Later, since the Katipuneros did not possess a single piece of firearm, they continued their activities to besieging the town of Daet. The Spaniards on the other hand, satisfied themselves with sporadic sniping from vantage point such as the windows and roof of the house of Arana.

The native civil guards inside the house of Arana were unable to carry out the assignment given to them by Moreno. Since the very beginning of the siege, they were stationed by Lt. Correa far apart from each other. Moreover, there was at least one-armed Spaniard behind each one of them watchful of their every move.

The Spaniards also restored to the ruse of telling the native civil guards that they had heard the siren of a steamboat from Nueva Caceres bringing reinforcement and coming to their rescue.

Moreno waited In vain that day for the native civil guards to revolt from within the house of Arana and turn their guns to the Spaniards.

Martyrs' Chapter VI: The Events of the 16th Day of April

The morning of April 16 found Daet under control of the Katipuneros who completely surrounded the house of Arana where the Spaniards were defending themselves.

The Katipuneros occupied the building of ihe Court of First Instance near the southern end of the old Spanish bridge. From there, they challenge the Spaniards holed inside the house of Arana. The Katipuneros also freed the prisoners of the public jail and imprisoned the warden. He was later rescued by the Spaniards at the end of the siege.

A new plan of attack was adopted to be carried out that evening. The Katipuneros would launch another attack, at which point the native civil guards inside the house of Arana would fire at the Spaniards, seize their arms and take over the place.

The agreed signal for the start of thr attack was the firing of a cannon, which the Katipuneros had seized from the convent in Daet. If the civil guards did not answer in any way, the cannon would he fired a second time.

Moreno was inside the house of Arana for the purpose of leading the native civil guards in the intended plan. He had gone there pretending to be loyal to the Spaniards.

But the plan was discovered by the Spaniards. Moreno was subdued by them, tied and placed under guard so that he would not be able to give any warning to the native civil guards. The Spaniards then prepared for the attack.

Lt. Correa ordered the native civil guards to rest until 12:00 that evening. Then he gathered their arms and handed them over to the Spaniards. Half of the civil guards were thus disarmed.

At about 7:30 in the evening, the first signal of the attack came The Katipuneros fired their first cannon shot   which hit the roof of the house of Arana. They also rang the church bells.   The   Spaniards fired back.

Sensing that the   native civil   guards did   not answer to the agreed signals, the Katipuneros again loaded and fired their cannons.

At that moment, the Spaniards grappled with the native civil guards. Outnumbered, the tatter were easily overcome. Seven of them were tied and the others were killed. One of the guards was able to escape with a gun by jumping out or the window and hiding among the shrubs. He later related to the Katipuneros what had happened inside the house of Arana.

Meanwhile, Lt. Correa had climbed up the flat roof of the Arana house where **Moreno** was tied. Upon hearing the signal of the cannon shot, Lt. Correa seized his revolver and fired twice at **Moreno.** Shortly after, he shot **Gabino/11/,** another leader of the Katipuneros and a former *capitan municipal* who had joined Moreno inside the house of Arana as part of the plot.

Not contented, Lt. Correa looked for the civil guards. Seeing one, he shot and killed him.

That evening, the floor of the Arana house was spattered with the blood of the martyrs **Moreno, Gabino** and several of the native civil guards.

At dawn of the next day, their corpses were carried down to the yard where they were burned and buried in a common grave. An eyewitness wrote: *"those killed first were brought down to the fire but were not consumed. It was very painful to see the dogs entertained in the remains. Even the besieged eat human flesh during these days. To avoid further complication: it was determined to burn all the corpses in a hole dug out for the purpose. The remains not consumed by the fire were emitting bad odor and to remedy that, we collected everything left over and burned it with the newly dead."* (Translated from the origina Spanish)

Martyrs' Chapter VII: Events of the 17th Day of April

The steamboat *Serrantes* arrived at Barra from Nueva Caceres with reinforcement consisting of a force of 21 civil guards led by **Captain Abreu** and another Spanish Officer.

The Katipuneros tried to repulse the new arrivals. They placed their cannons at the road and fired at the Spanish troops. Their efforts, however, were futile as Captain Abreu and his force managed to reach Daet at about 2:30 in the afternoon and to rescue the beleaguered Spaniards in the house of Arana.

/11/ *Possibly, he was* **Gavino Saavedra.**

Additional reinforcement of 150 troops arrived, under the command of **Sgt. Pegerto Lopez** and a certain **Sgt Narciso**. They had encountered and fought earlier that day some Katipuneros in the municipality of Talisay, where ihey killed the town's capitan municipal and a certain man named Luzon.

Thus reinforced, the Spaniards took the offensive in Daet. They drove the Katipuneros from the houses and trenches they still occupied and hunted them down, killing more titan thirty that afternoon.

That same afternoon of April 17, Capt. Abreu decided that all those who had revolted and joined the uprising be executed. He made known his decision only to Lt Correa and some Spaniards.

In the evening, the first executions were carried out under cover of darkness. Lt. Correa called the corporals who had come with Capt. Abreu from Nueva Caceres and Siro Mirablanca and ordered them to take charge of the beheading. Mirablanca refused to take part in the execution. Sgt. Narciso took his place and, together with two corporals, beheaded the remaining native civil guards of DM on the roof of the house of Arana.

The corpses were then thrown from the roof into the street where they were buried the following day

Martyrs' Chapter VIII: Subsequents Events of April

The Spaniards regain control of Daet on April 18. A Holy Mass was celebrated by **Frav Antonio Mirablanca** which was attended only by the Spaniards.   The Filipino inhabitants of' Daet were not present.

In the afternoon of that day, the Spanish authorities issued a decree ordering the residents to come down from their houses and those who hid fled to return to Daet. They were told that they had nothing to fear and that no reprisal or punishment would be inflected or them.

However the Spaniards arrested the leaders and members of the Katipunan and even those who were merely suspected by them. Many were executed.

Among those put to death during the first week following the collapse of the revolt were *capitan municipal* **Jose Abano** and former *capitanes municipal* **Tomas Zaldua and Domingo Lozada**. Abano and Lozada were tortured; the former was afterwards thrown into a well while still alive **Aniceto Gregorio,** together with **six other Filipinos,** were reported to have been burned alive in the plaza. Others were bayoneted to death.

Martyrs Chapter IX: Events of the Following Months

On the first day of May, the steamboat *Montanes* arrived at the port of Barra with 50 members of the recently organized Rural Guides on board. They were sent by Spanish Captain General and commanded by First Lt. Alfredo Damelt.

Upon their being stationed in Daet, the Spanish military authorities formed a *Tribunal de Cuchillo/12/.* This tribunal or committee took charge of passing sentence without trial on the suspected katipuneros and their sympathizers.

Daily arrest were made. Most were incarcerated in the local jail, and the test were put in the ground floor of the house of Arana. There they awaited the sentence of death pronounced by the committee. The executions were carried out by the soldiers of the Rural Guides, who either shot, beheaded or bayoneted the victims.

Other prominent townsmen who were put to death were **Rosalio Pajarillo** and **Jacinto Rada,** officials of the Court of First Instance of Daet, **Isodoro Avila,** a school teacher; **Andres Dames** and **Andres Obana**, clerks of the Court of First Instance, **Valentin Lipana,** vaccinator; **Domingo Lozada**, former *capitan municipal* of Daet; **Agaton Osias**, proprietor; **Leoncio Carranceja**, **Angel**

Zaleta, **Teodoro Zaleta** and **Pedro Amorsolo**, students; **Sixto Santa Catalina**, Justice of the Peace of Calasgasan; **Joaquin Moreno,** cousin of **Ildefonso Moreno**; **Gregorio del Valle** and **Florante Bacerdo.**

/I2/ *"Committee of Executions"*

Andres Dames, Andres Obana and **Vicente Salveria** were killed on the road to Basud. They had been ordered to go with a patrol of Rural Guides. Once outside the town of Daet, they were ordered to dismount their horses and were then shot in the back.

The Rural guides continued to hunt down the remnants of the Katipunan. Suspected Katipuneros were arrested and killed in nearby towns. In the latter part of June, the Rural Guides made an expedition to the islands of Canimog and Caringo, where some of the katipuneros had hidden. There they found and killed several of the latter.

Other Filipinos who suffered either arrest, torture or death were **Eugenio Boac, Santiago Ellaga, Esteban Imperial, Armando Mallare, Leoncio Montes, Roman Pajarillo, Florante Samante, Felix Vana, Eleuterio Zaleta, Arcadio Varga, Leoncio Avila, Valentin Cabanela, Severo Bernabe, Gregorio Luyon, Ceferino Millares, Leopoldo Nadal, Vicente Perez y Gonzales, Claro Pimentel, Anianas Salveria** and **Diego Linan.**

By the end of August 1898. the *Tribunal de Cuchillo* ordered the arrest of the last batch of victims. These were **Florentino Yaneza, Valeriano Calleja, Teodoro Banan,** and **Severo Banan.** They were kept imprisoned until the following month.

Earlier in August, **General Vicente Lukban** had overrun the Spanish force in the Southern Tagalog and, upon order of **General Agttinaldo**, proceeded to the Bicol Region. The Spaniards in Camarines Norte informed of the advancing forces **General Lukban**, decided to abandon the province. The first group of evacuees was the friars and some or the Spaniards.

On September 8, the forces of **General Lukban** landed at *Mambulao/13/* and Paracale. That same day. the Spaniards boarded the Norwegian steamboat *Vigdo* at the port of Barra and left for Hongkong. The next day, a second group of Spaniards took passage on the steamboat *Montanes* for N'ueva Caceres.

/13/ Now the municipality of Jose Panganiban

On September 12, upon learning that the advance units of General Lukban's army had reach the outskirts of barrio Matangco of the town of *lndan/14/* and moving towards Daet, the remaining Spanish functionaries and Rural Guides fled to Barra where the *Serrantes* had just docked that morning. They brought with them, the last four Filipino prisoners condemned by the *"tribunal de Cuchillo"*. Before sailing for lloilo, they bayoneted them to death.

Valeriano Cuano, a former *capitan municipal,* took charge of the government of Daet. When General Lukban arrived in Daet that same month of September. Cuano turned over the reins of government to him.

General Lukban proceeded to Nueva Caceres with his army, leaving a garrison in Daet under the command of **Captain Antonio Sanz**. It was during the command of Sanz that the first monument in honor of the national hero, Dr. Jose Rizal, was erected in Daet on December 30, 1898

Martyrs Chapter IX: Significance of Daet Revolt

In all outward appearance, the Daet Revolt ended in total defeat for the Filipinos and victory for the Spaniards.

Nonetheless, that uprising was the first burst of flames of the revolutionary ferment sweeping the Bicol region. The event of that fateful month of April 1898 signaled the beginning of the end of Spanish colonial authority in the region. Perhaps nothing could have expressed that message more forcefully than the image of the last four martyrs sprawled lifeless on the docks of Barra and in the distant horizon fleeing Spaniards on board the steamboat *Serrantes.*

/14/ Now the municipality Vinzons

Sources

1.   **Interviews**: (a) Dolores A. Camilar, (b) Antonio R. Abano, (c) Igmedio Zaldua, (d) Other known descendants of the Camarines Norte Martyrs.

2.   **Documents from**: (a) National Archives (b) Abano Family Records

3.   **Books:** (a) Juan Elias Ataviado, *The Philippine Revolution in the Bicol Region, August 1896-January 1899* (Manila, 1953); (b) Fray Marcos Gomez, O.F.M., *La Revolution Filipina de 1898 en Ambos Camarines*, Translated by Fray Apolinar Pastrana (Manila, Regal Printing Co., 1980); (c) Rey Imperial, *Revolutionary Career of Vicente Lukban*, A Doctoral Thesis (U.P. Department of History), (d) Danilo M. Gerona, *From Epic History: A Brief Introduction to Bicol History* (Naga City, AMS Press, 1988).

Originally printed by Mabini College Computer Services Center, with Costs appropriated by Office of Cong. Jess B. Pimentel.

2

The Self-Perpetuating Elite of the Philippines

Rodel Rodis

In the July 1968 issue of the American magazine *Foreign Affairs*, a novice Filipino senator introduced his country to the American people as "a land in which a few are spectacularly rich while the masses remain abjectly poor. . . . a land consecrated to democracy but run by an entrenched plutocracy... a people whose ambitions run high, but whose fulfillment is low and mainly restricted to the self-perpetuating elite...a land of privilege and rank – a republic dedicated to equality but mired in an archaic system of caste."

http://www.foreignaffairs.com/articles/24006/benigno-s-aquino-jr/whats-wrong-with-the-philippines

The young senator should have also shared his insights with the Filipino people ashis thoughtful essay should also have been published in the Philippines and should have been required reading in Philippine schools. It still should be, even now - 46 years later.

The young author was Sen. Benigno "Ninoy" Aquino, Jr., a member of the "entrenched plutocracy" and the "self-perpetuating elite" of the Philippines.

Ninoy Aquino came from a "prosperous family of hacenderos" (Wikipedia), a family which gained prominence when his grandfather, Servillano Aquino, served as a general in Pres. Emilio Aguinaldo's Revolutionary Army. Aquino's father Benigno Aquino, Sr. was elected to the Philippine House of Representatives in 1919 before winning a Philippine Senate seat in 1928, the first of many Aquinos to be elected to the Senate including Ninoy, his son Noynoy, his siblings Butz and Tess, and his nephew Bam.

While Aquino was the youngest Filipino politician ever to be elected mayor (at age 22), governor (at age 29) and senator (at age 34), he never got to be the country's youngest president because Marcos declared martial law in 1972 voiding the 1973 presidential elections where Aquino was favored to win. While Aquino never became president because of his assassination in 1983, his widow, Cory, and his son, Noynoy, were both elected to the country's top post.

ORIGIN OF THE S.P.E.

The origin of the "self-perpetuating elite" of the Philippines can be traced to the decision of the Spanish colonizers in the third century of their rule to appoint the most prominent local Ilustrados in each town and province as gobernadorcillos to collect taxes from the people.

When the Americans colonized the Philippines at the turn of the 20th century, they continued the Spanish colonial practice and appointed local Ilustrados to political positions as well.

Uncomplicated Mind blogger Joe Rivera wrote: "When the U.S. colonized the Philippines at the turn of the 20th century, they took these Ilustrados under their wings and trained them for the practical affairs of popular government. The first American civil governor of the islands, William Howard Taft, believed that the rudiments of self-government would easily be transferable to these Ilustrados, the oligarchic elite, because of their social and economic status. So, it was the fault of the American colonizers that spawned the political dynasties we have now."

In every province of the Philippines, political power was wielded by the local Ilustrados who kept political power limited to their families making the surnames Osmena, Lopez, Cojuangco, Roxas, Aquino, Macapagal and Marcos household names in Philippine politics.

Rivera described the consequence of Taft's Ilustrado policy: "Taft's idea of letting society's affluent members constitute the Philippine Assembly in 1907 and Congress in the ensuing years resulted in the formation and circulation of elites that perpetuate their hold on political offices. A truly representative democracy failed to flourish, shattering the hopes that the country would now be able to draw upon all classes in Philippine society in electing public officials."

As Carlos Conde noted in his New York Times article, *Family dynasties bind politics in the Philippines*, (May 11, 2007), "political dynasties were an offshoot of the country's colonial experience, in which the Filipino elite was nurtured by Spanish and American colonizers. Even after the country gained independence, in 1946, the largely feudal system persisted, as landed Filipino families sought to protect their interests by occupying public offices."

Conde added: "There are an estimated 250 political families nationwide, with at least one in every province, occupying positions in all levels of the bureaucracy... Of the 265 members of Congress, 160 belong to these clans."

According to one estimate, 40 percent of provincial congressmen and governors are related, and 50 percent of both are related to previous holders of those offices.

"These are the same families who belong to the country's economic elite, some of them acting as rule makers or patrons of politicians who conspire together to amass greater economic power," said Roberto Tuazon, director of the Center for People Empowerment in Governance.

NON-ILUSTRADO ELITE

But even when a political figure with no ties to the traditional Ilustrado elite emerges, he quickly develops the impulse to amass and perpetuate political power in his family.

An example is Joseph Ejercito who was born to an upper middle class family in Tondo, Manila, and who became a popular movie actor under his screen name,"Joseph Estrada", after he was expelled from Ateneo University. He parlayed his fame as an actor to be elected mayor of San Juan, a post from which he then ran for and was elected variously as senator, vice-president and then as president in 1998.

After Estrada was removed from office in 2001 by "People Power II", his first wife, Dr. Loi Ejercito, was elected to the senate, followed by one son, Jinggoy, and yet another son, J.V. Ejercito. His nephew, ER Ejercito (real name George Estregan, Jr.) was elected Laguna governor in 2010 (although he may soon be removed from office for "overspending"). Even after a plunder conviction and a sentence of life imprisonment, "Erap" Estrada managed somehow to be elected mayor of Manila in 2013.

Like Estrada, the man widely assumed to be the next president of the Philippines, Vice-President Jejomar "Jojo" Binay, also did not descend from the Ilustrado elite. Orphaned at nine years old, Binay was adopted by his uncle, Ponciano, a man of modest means. Binay studied at regular local schools before acquiring a law degree from the University of the Philippines. As a lawyer, Binay volunteered to provide free legal assistance to victims of human rights abuses during the Marcos dictatorship.

Because he was an ardent supporter of Cory Aquino in the 1986 People Power Uprising, Binay (later known as "Rambotito") was rewarded with an appointment as mayor of Makati in 1986. He was elected in his own right in 1988, then reelected in 1992 and 1995 when term limits required him to relinquish the post to his wife, Elenita Binay, who was elected mayor in 1995. Binay was elected mayor again 1998 and again until 2010 when he ran and won as Vice-President.

FILIPINOS VOTE FOR FAMILY, NOT CLASS OR IDEOLOGY

Since Binay's mayoral appointment in 1986, Makati has known no other mayor not named Binay. After he was elected VP in 2010, his son, Jejomar Erwin "JunJun" Binay, Jr., succeeded him as mayor. One daughter, Mar-Len "Abigail" Binay is a House member representing Makati while another daughter, Nancy, was elected to the Senate in 2013 despite having absolutely no prior job experience other than as her father's "executive assistant".

Conde observed that members of dynasties, like the emerging Binay Dynasty of Makati, have "developed a sense of entitlement regarding public positions" as evidenced by Makati Mayor JunJun Binay order to arrest three Dasmarinas Village security guards who were not aware that the mayor of Makati is exempt from complying with rules for ordinary citizens not allowed to pass through certain gates past a certain hour. What is unfortunate is that "many ordinary Filipinos accept the (entitlement) arrangement as inevitable, which makes it difficult to change the situation."

https://www.youtube.com/watch?v=ojFGo9RN5mY

In his widely-read 1988 essay, A Damaged Culture, James Fallows wrote: "when observing Filipino friendships I thought often of the Mafia families portrayed in The Godfather: total devotion to those within the circle, total war on those outside. Because the boundaries of decedent treatment are limited to the family or tribe, they exclude at least 90 percent of the people in the country."

Anthropologist Brian Fegan asserts in his book, "*An Anarchy of Families: State and Family in the Philippines*", that Filipinos tend not to vote according to class, ethnicity, religion or even ideology. They vote for family which has become "the most enduring political unit and the one into which, failing some wider principle of participation, all other units dissolve."

The system of family clan dominance is a vicious cycle, Political Science Prof. Julio Teehankee asserts, because it "prevents the expansion of the base of aspirants and candidates for representation." The result, he added, is a political system dominated by patronage, corruption, violence, and fraud.

CLAN DOMINANCE

The dominance of the family clans has prevented the flowering of democracy in the Philippines.

"Continuing clan dominance is a product of the seemingly immutable and unequal socioeconomic structure, as well as the failure to develop a truly democratic electoral and party system," said Prof. Teehankee (quoted by Conde).

The system is a vicious cycle, one that prevents the expansion of the base of aspirants and candidates for representation, Teehankee said. The result, he added, is a political system dominated by patronage, corruption, violence, and fraud.

This is the political system that has produced fixers like Janet Lim Napoles who conspired with the dynasts in Congress to steal taxpayer money intended to provide the people with much needed services and infrastructure improvements.

Among the senators disclosed by Napoles as having received billions of pesos of kickbacks from her pork barrel scams are past and present senators including: Juan Ponce-Enrile, Jinggoy Estrada, Bong

Revilla, Gringo Honasan, Loren Legarda, Loi Ejercito, Vic Sotto, Rodolfo Biazon, Tessie Aquino-Oreta, Ferdinand "Bongbong" Marcos, Jr., Manny Villar, Chiz Escudero, Cynthia Villar, Aquilino "Koko" Pimentel, Jr., Aquilino "Nene" Pimentel Sr., Alan Peter Cayetano and Lito Lapid.

Not all the "self-perpetuating elite" of the Philippines conspired with Napoles but all those who did were certified members of the "self-perpetuating elite".

(Send comments to Rodel50@gmail.com or mail them to the Law Offices of Rodel Rodis at 2429 Ocean Avenue, San Francisco, CA 94127 or call 415.334.7800).

3

Isang Open Letter Tungkol sa Trapiko
By Ragulane

Alam naming hindi madali ang inyong trabaho, alam naming hindi madaling patinuin ang mga motoristang salbahe at walang respeto sa kalsada at alam din naming sumasakit na ang inyong ulo sa kung ano at papaano ang susunod ninyong istratehiya upang maibsan o mabawasan man lang ang lumalalang traffic situation sa Kamaynilaan. Pero alam naming merong kayong police powers and authority para disiplinahin ang napakaraming pasaway sa kalsada kaya kayo lang ang may kapangyarihan na maisaayos sa legal na paraan ang maligalig at magulong sitwasyon ng trapiko dito sa atin. Hindi katulad namin na simpleng mamamayan lang ng republikang aming kinabibilangan.

Kung talagang seryoso kayo na mapaluwag ang trapiko sa Kalakhang Maynila hindi lang dapat number coding ang mahigpit niyong ipinatutupad, maaaring makatulong sa pagluwag ng daloy ng trapiko ang pagpapatupad ng daytime truck ban pero malaking dagok naman ito sa ating ekonomiya at 'di lang natin gaanong pansin na apektado tayo nito.

May dahilan kung bakit nagpatayo ng napakaraming footbridge sa Kamaynilaan pero kapansin-pansin ang mga pedestrian na mas ninanais na tumawid sa ilalim nito (talamak ito sa kanto ng

Abad Santos Ave. at Recto). Bakit hinahayaan ng mga magigiting ninyong traffic enforcers ang mga walang disiplinang pedestrian na ito na daan-daanan lang sila?

Takot ba sila na ipatupad ang batas?

O sumuko na rin sila sa kasasaway sa mga jaywalkers?

Masikip na nga ang kalsada sumasabay pa ang mga mababait na pedestriang ito. Kung ganoon pala bakit gumastos pa tayo ng milyon-milyong pisong halaga ng footbridges gayong masaya naman ang lahat na nakikipaglaro ng patintero sa rumaragasang iba't ibang sasakyan.

Baka nakakalimutan ng inyong opisina na hindi pa pinapayagan ang pedicab, tricycle at kuliglig sa mga main road (DILG Memo Circular 2007-01, Local Gov't Code Sec. 447 & 458) kaya muli namin itong ipinapaalala sa inyo.

Pero bakit nagkalat sila sa ating mga pangunahing kalsada?

Mga pedicab/kuliglig na nakikipag-unahan sa lahat ng uri ng sasakyan at may pasaherong lampas pa sa kayang isakay ng ordinaryong taxi, mga tricycle na kaliwa't kanan kung mag-cut at mag-overtake na tila ayaw na nauungusan. Idagdag pa natin na ang mga ito ay walang prangkisa, hindi napipigilan ang pagdami, walang pakundangan sa pagmamaneho, walang pakialam sa batas trapiko at ang nakapagtataka ay hindi sila sinisita man lang ng mga opisyal ng alinmang traffic agencies o sinumang traffic enforcers. Hindi masama ang magtrabaho pero hindi ba't ang batas ay ginawa at ipinatutupad para sa lahat?

Hari ng kalsada kung sila'y ituring, bakit nga ba hindi eh wala silang respeto sa kapwa nila motorista. Magsasakay at magbababa sa kahit saang lugar nila naisin, bigla na lang hihimpil at maghihintay sa pasaherong sampung kanto pa ang layo, hihinto sa pinakagitna ng kalsada kesehodang siya ang maging sanhi ng pagkabuhol-buhol na trapiko. Mga PUJ na akala mo'y asong gala na tatae na lang kung saan sila abutan, ayaw magbigay daan at sila pang galit kung iyong pagsasabihan. Tulad ng mga tricycle/ pedicab/ kuliglig driver may laya rin silang huminto kahit berde ang ilaw at aarangkada kahit na ito'y pula. Siyempre hindi naman lahat ng jeepney driver ay violator meron din namang matitino at panakanaka ay sumusunod sa batas trapiko pero ilang porsyento lang kaya sila?

Sana. Sana lang ay mabigyang tuldok na ninyo ang lantarang paglabag ng mga astig na driver na ito.

Lahat na yata ng pagdidisiplina ay ginawa na ng inyong opisina sa mga unstoppable at higanteng mga buses pero tulad ng dati hindi sila nagpapatinag at nagpapaapekto sa anumang sanction at parusang kaya ninyong ipataw sa kanila. Kahit na kitang-kita naman na sila ang malaking bahagi nang dahilan ng pagsimula ng trapik kung saan sila bumibyahe o rumurota.

Dalawang dambuhalang bus lang ang nakabalagbag sa kalsada ay tiyak nang makagagawa ng kilometrong pagsikip ng trapiko.

Pero kahit libong beses n'yo man silang pagmultahin, suspendihin o alisan ng prangkisa sana 'wag kayong huminto sa pagdisiplina sa kanila.

Sa inyong kaalaman baka walang nag-iinform sa inyong opisina na:

- Maraming lugar sa Kalakhang Maynila kabilang na ang kahabaan ng A.Bonifacio Ave. mula Quezon City hanggang Lungsod ng Maynila ay tila pangkaraniwan na lang ang mga sasakyang nagka-counterflow; mula kuliglig o tricyle hanggang sa magagarang sasakyan, nandun sila sa tapat mismo ng North Cemetery makakakapal ang mukhang binabalandra ang kanilang kawalang galang. Ganito rin ang senaryong ginagawa ng mga motor at tricycle sa Fourth Avenue sa Caloocan City at sa Bonifacio Drive at R-10 sa Maynila at Caloocan.

- Lantarang ginagawang (ilegal) terminal ng mga tricycle o jeepney driver ang mga pangunahing kalsada na sa obvious na dahilan ay pinapayagan ng mga pulis at traffic enforcers. Sa A. Mabini St. sa Pajo, Caloocan, sa ilalim ng LRT partikular ang Abad Santos at sa R. Papa stations ay ilan sa mga halimbawa nito. Kung bakit naman din kasi pinapayagan ng kung sino na ang isang kalsada ay isara para sa liga ng basketball ay sila lang ang nakakaalam. Kaya hayun, dagdag sakit ng ulo sa inyo at sa amin.

- Bukod sa illegal terminal ng tricycle at jeepney, malaking perwisyo rin ang mga vendor at ang mga nakapark sa mga main road at secondary road. Hindi lingid sa inyo at sa atin na noong kapanahunan ni Chairman BF ay halos nasawata na ito pero ngayon tila umarangkada na naman ang mga illegal vendors at illegally parked vehicles sa halos lahat ng lugar sa Kamaynilaan. Sa Dangwa na bagsakan at bilihan ng mga murang bulaklak ay masikip ang trapiko kahit sa dis-oras ng gabi at ang dahilan nito ay ang mga nakapark na iba't ibang uri ng sasakyan; delivery van, mga sasakyan ng mamimili, at private vehicle ng mga stall owner. Samantalang sa magkabilang kanto ay hindi bababa sa tatlong traffic enforcer ang nakatalaga para magmando ng trapiko, galing 'di ba? Nilalaparan ba ng DPWH ang kalsada para gawing paradahan lang ng mga pribadong sasakyan?

Higit sa isandaang milyong na ang populasyon natin at napakalaking labingdalawang porsyentong Pilipino (more or less) ay nakakalat sa Kalakhang Maynila habang nasa siyam na milyon ang nakatalang nakarehistrong sasakyan sa LTO, hindi pa kabilang dito ang daang-libong mga sasakyang walang rehistro. Walang eksaktong numero kung ilang sasakyan ang naglipana sa Metro Manila pero tiyak na milyong bilang rin ito na nakikipagsiksikan at nakikipag-gitgitan sa malasardinas na kalsada ng Kamaynilaan. Kaya kung susumahin namin ang inyong trabaho siguradong resulta nito ay matinding sakit ng ulo.

Milyong sasakyan + masikip na kalsada + walang disiplinang motorista at pedestrian + baha sa tuwing maulan + inconsistent/unreliable traffic enforcer = Teribleng Trapiko.

Totoo ngang sa ikauunlad ng bayan ay disiplina ang kailangan. Subok na ito ngunit bakit hindi natin ito kayang i-apply sa ating sarili dahil magmula sa pinakamahirap na motorista hanggang sa mga taong may matataas na katungkulan sa pamahalaan ay tila walang pakundangang nilalapastangan ang batas sa lansangan.

Hanggang saan ba ang pagtitiis naming ito?

Hihintayin pa ba nating bansagan ng mga dayuhan, na ang kalsada ng Kamaynilaan ay "Roads of Hell"?

Hahayaan na lang ba nating babuyin at walanghiyain ng marami ang nakalatag na batas trapiko?

Ano na naman kaya ang susunod ninyong ipagbabawal sa kalsada?

Ano ba ang inyong susunod na komprehensibong plano upang lumuwag ang kalsada?

Kung iisipin at tutuusin, hindi natin kinakailangan ng karagdagan pang plano, polisiya o batas para maibsan ang masikip na traffic na araw-araw nating nararanasan dahil sapat na ang umiiral na mga regulasyon at batas. Dagdagan niyo lang sana ng kahigpitan at lagyan ng ngipin ang pagpapatupad nito sa lahat ng uri ng mamamayan mapamahirap o mayaman man ito. Sigurado, unti-unting magkakaroon ito ng progreso.

At kami bilang ordinaryong motorista at pasahero ay susunod, makikipagkoordinasyon at makikipag - kooperasyon sa lahat ng pagkakataon para sa ikabubuti at kapakanan ng mas nakararami.

Hindi na siguro namin kailangan sabihin pa na ang katumbas ng bawat oras na pagkaantala sa traffic ay milyon ang halaga, hindi na siguro namin kailangang sabihin pa na may mga taong nagbuwis na ng buhay dahil sa pagkaburyong sa traffic, hindi na siguro namin kailangang sabihin pa na nagpapabagal sa pag-unlad ng ekonomiya ang traffic. Siguradong alam ninyo 'yan kaya nga kayo itinalaga at iniluklok sa posisyong hawak ninyo dahil sa malawak ninyong karanasan at kaalaman.

Maraming Salamat at sana'y mabigyang pansin ninyo ang bukas na liham na ito.

Lubos na umaasa,

Mga naiinip na motorista

4

Truest Yet Rendered Death Ode of Rizal
By Robert M. Bernardo, 2014

To PH, Globe, Cause, Creed; by him finished, smuggled
out twice in lamp and shoes, enacted 12/30/1896. This
2014 revision of a 1896 one is by Robert M. Bernardo
of cnx.org free ebook on this.

Adios Patria adorada, Land loved of Sun,
A pearl in seas of the Orient, our lost Eden!
I leave happy to give you this sad faded life:
And were it more brilliant, more fresh, more flourishing
Still I'd give it for you, give it for your need's sake.

In camps of battle fighting there In delirium
Others give you their lives with no doubts, no remorse.
Places don't matter, cypress, laurel, lily fields,
Gallows, vast plains, combat cruel martyrdom.
They are the same when needed by Homeland and
home.

I die upon seeing the sky's colors bursting
At last announcing day through the cowl of gloom.
If dye you want to redden more your daylight glow
Pour out my blood, disperse it in most fitting time.
And gild it with radiance from your rising sunrise!

Dreams of mine since a boy, hardly adolescent,
Dreams of mine since youth surged inside me with
vigor.
They longed to see you yet be gem of Orient Seas:
Those dusky eyes not in tears, your head held upright
Face with no frowns no furrows and none of shame's
stains!

Obsession of my life, its live ardent longings:
"Salud!," salutes to you this soul now to depart;
"Salud!," ahh... what beauty to fall pushing your flight;
To die to give you life, to die beneath your skies;
To sleep in your enchanted land eternally.

You may someday see spring to life at my gravesite,
Amidst thick grassy weeds, simple flower humble.
Approach, go brush your lips on it to kiss my soull
Then I on face in my cold tomb would also feel
The touch of your tenderness, the heat of your breath.

Wish moon to watch over me in soft light tranquil;
Let dawn parade displays of passing resplendence.
Let the winds howl—moan with murmurous gravity.
If some songbird flies down to display on my cross,
You wish it to intone its canticles of peace.

Watch burning sun make our poured rains evaporate,
Pure back to skies—sigh too clamors mine would
follow!
Let fellow friend my quite early ending decry
But in serene late noon when one for me might pray,
Wish also 0 Nativeland for my rest in God.

Pray for legions dying but not finding fortune;
For all those enduring torments beyond compare.
For poor grieving mothers wailing their bitterest;
For orphans, widows, prisoners under torture:
And pray for self that your final redemption looms!

Then when the black of night shrouds the cemetery
And the dead only they are left there to themselves,
Don't disturb their sleep don't disturb the mystery.
Maybe now you hear chords from some old lyre or
lute?
It's I loved Patria I, who would yet sing to you!

In time my grave may even grow to be unknown,
Not bearing cross nor headstone to mark location.
Let workman plow all that's left with spade dispersing.
What's spread out there before it turns into nothing?
Powder in your carpet of earth you let it form!

Therefore, matters not that you'd place me in limbo.
Your atmosphere, your space, valleys I'll sweep my
way.
Vibrant and pure notes I'll keep voicing in your ears,
Aromas, lights, colors, rumors, songs, sorrows:
Constant, there repeating essence of my own faith.

My idolized Patria, pain of my many pains,
Loved Philippines: you listen to this last farewell!
I leave you everything, my parents and loved ones.
I go where none are slavers killers oppressors:
Where faith does not kill...where rule obeys God's own.

Adios, parents and family: chunks of my soul;
Friends in infancy from the homes that we all lost.
Give thanks at last I rest from this fatiguing day!
Goodbye sweet foreigner, my friend, my contentment
Farewell my loved fellow beings: with death goes rest!

[Read as such eve-of-death ode in 1902 by Rep. Henry Cooper to an imperial U.S. Congress; awed, ft granted PH calibrated autonomy into Independence in 1946.]

From its historic eve-of-death fame, this unique document-poem's progress towards recognition as a great world cultural legacy was later blocked and confused by partisanship, this by antedating its finishing-and-smuggling date and how these were done. Corresponding reinterpretations and mistranslations followed, a national artist's hailed but very poor one just one of a kind. None of them stood by highly researched true dates on points above. Nor did they strictly render the original's Alexandrine lines in iambic hexameter, though exact end-rhyming patterns could not be replicated, given the primacy of literal fidelity.

This Is then the "Truest Yet Rendering". It is the only version by which Filipinos can fathom fully this summing-up death legacy of their acknowledged Greatest One, Spanish not being , accessible to them and Tagalog unable to do the job as well. Hence some of you 'do-gooders' may want to reprint this on your own to share widely with them and others. Keep

all the profits if you decide selling it. Some "Don't Do Evil Googlers" may help, such as this one below, for which thanks.
— rbernardo2@yahoo.com

5

Aquino SONA 2014: PNoy's 5th SONA Full Transcript (English version)

SONA of Noynoy Aquino for 2014, his 5th State of the Nation Address (SONA) since he became the Philippine President, was delivered today, July 28, 2014, at the Session Hall of the House of Representatives in Batasang Pambansa Complex, Quezon City.

Below is the full transcript of PNoy's SONA 2014, which was 44-page long and lasted for an hour and a half (1 hour and 34 minutes

Vice President Jejomar Binay; President Fidel Valdez Ramos; Senate President Franklin M. Drilon and members of the Senate; Speaker Feliciano Belmonte Jr. and members of the House of Representatives; Chief Justice Maria Lourdes Sereno and our Justices of the Supreme Court; distinguished members of the diplomatic corps; members of the Cabinet; officials in local government; members of the military, police, and other uniformed services; my fellow public servants; and, to my Bosses, the Filipino people:

Good afternoon.

This is my fifth SONA; only one remains. We have a saying: Those who do not look back to the past, will never get to where they wish to go. Therefore, today it is only right for us to reflect on what we have gone through.

This was our situation in the past: To dream was an absurdity. We had a senseless bureaucracy; padded contracts had become the norm; and corruption was endemic to the system. We were known as the "Sick Man of Asia." The economy was weak; industry was sparse. We failed to gain the confidence of investors. The result: very few jobs were created. We found a people deprived of hope. Many of us had already given up, and were forced to take their chances in other countries. With heads bowed, we had come to accept that we would never be able to rely on our government or our society.

The Philippines sank deep into despair because of dirty politics.Our trust in each other disappeared; the confidence of the world in the Philippines ebbed, and worst of all: we lost faith in ourselves.

It was at this juncture that we began our journey on the straight and righteous path.

As the father of our nation, on my shoulders rest not only the problems that we inherited and the problems that arise today—it is also my duty to prepare for the future. At every moment, I must be mindful of the concerns and perspectives of all. Think about it this way: it is as if you are watching two hundred TV channels at the same time. You need to understand not just what is unfolding before you—you also need to know what happened before, and where it could all lead. Confusion is not an option, and you must have a response for every question, suggestion, and criticism—and you must have all the answers even before the questions are asked. This is not an easy job, and I am only human, one who at times is also capable of feeling apprehension.

In spite of this, my resolve is firm because my primary goal is clear: To return government to its rightful mandate—to serve the Filipino people always.

Is it not true that we have a saying: Give a man a fish and you feed him for a day. Teach a man to fish and you feed him for a lifetime. An example of this is the Technical Education and Skills Development Authority (TESDA). The Disbursement Acceleration Program contributed 1.6 billion pesos to TESDA's Training for Work Scholarship Program. This amount enabled the graduation of 223,615 beneficiaries. 66 percent of these—or, 146,731 graduates—now have jobs. As for the remaining 34 percent, TESDA is helping them find employment. Just take a look: All of these scholars have their names and other pertinent data listed down, should you wish to confirm them.

If we divide the allocated funding by the number of graduates, we will see that government invested around 7,155 pesos in every scholar. In the BPO sector, a monthly salary of 18,000 is already considered at the low end. Every year, he will earn 234,000 pesos. If he is given the maximum tax deduction, his annual income tax will be: 7,900 pesos. This means that in the first year alone the 7,155 pesos that the government invested in him would have been paid back—and there will even be a profit. This and all the taxes he will be paying the government until he retires will, in turn, provide his countrymen with the same opportunities he was given. This is good governance:

The right intentions, practices, and results. Everyone wins.

Let us listen to the stories of two TESDA graduates:

Translated transcript of Testimonial of Marc Joseph Escora, TESDA beneficiary:

Even when you've realized your dreams, you should know that success, it's still not stable. You still need to work hard for it.

I am Marc Joseph Escora. I am a high school graduate. Through the help of the Technical Education and Skills Development Authority [TESDA], I have my career in the business process outsourcing (BPO) industry right now. I was based in the Libertad public market for seven years. I worked as a barker forpublic transportation vehicles. My family couldn't afford to put all of us through school, so I needed to find a way to support myself, so I could graduate.

The most important thing I've learned is to have the confidence to interact with other people. When people see that you have a disability, they usually won't be able to see past it, to your abilities. So you need to trust yourself.

If TESDA wasn't there to help me, I probably wouldn't be where I am now. Our way of living now is much better than how we lived back then.

Translated transcript of Testimonial of Jonnalyn Navarossa, TESDA beneficiary

TESDA helped me finish my studies, find a job, and support my family.

I am Jonnalyn Navarossa, Technical Trainer at Toyota Motor Philippines. I graduated top of Batch 1 of automotive servicing training class at TESDA Region 4-A. I chose to study automotive servicing because I've always dreamed of being a mechanical engineer. In order for me to both earn a living and save up, I enrolled at TESDA.

We're used to thinking that being an auto mechanic is a man's job. But I've proven that as long you work hard, as long as you're determined, we can ensure quality products. TESDA taught me the value of good, clean, and quality work.

Now, I'm more confident in myself. And it's much easier to dream bigger.

We launched the Expanded Conditional Cash Transfer Program in June of 2014, with a budget of 12.3 billion pesos. Now, the government will also support the beneficiaries until they are 18 years old. Some will ask, "Why?" According to a study conducted by the Philippine Institute for Development Studies, a high school graduate earns 40 percent more than someone who was only able to finish grade school.

We are investing in our most valuable resource: The Filipino people. Data from the National Economic Development Authority attests to our success. According to them, the 27.9 percent poverty rate during the first semester of 2012 went down to 24.9 percent for the same period in 2013. These three percentage points are equivalent to 2.5 million Filipinos who have crossed the poverty line.

Of course, it is only right that we focus on the needs of the poorest in our society. But we will not stop there. Now that we have greater resources, we are striving to ensure that all those who crossed the poverty line will never go back below it.

When we came into office, we found a society that was like a derelict house in which we had no choice but to live. What was even worse: we had virtually no tools and materials with which to repair the damage. Over the past few years, with the help of every Filipino who cared for the well-being of his fellowmen, we have been acquiring the tools and materials we need. One of these tools is a budget focused solely on the needs of the citizenry—a budget we have passed on-time four years in a row. These tools include the laws that have accelerated the bringing of benefits to our bosses.

This is where—under a fair system—the resurgence of our economy began. We were able to save because of prudent fiscal management. We were able to expand the coverage of essential services without raising taxes, apart from Sin Tax reform, whose goal is to reduce vice in society.

We worked to have the ability to fund the projects that we implemented, are implementing, and will be implementing. We strengthened tax collections: from 1.094 trillion pesos in collections in 2010, we increased this to 1.536 trillion pesos in 2013. [Applause]

We improved the management of our debt. The result: a decrease in our debt to GDP ratio; money that once went to paying interest, we were able to channel into social services. We were even able to fulfill the obligations of government that we inherited from past administrations. For example: In 1993, or during the administration of President Ramos, the government was required to recapitalize the Central Bank of the Philippines with 50 billion pesos, so that it could fulfill its mandate. President Ramos was able to fund 10 billion pesos and nothing was added since then. 40 billion pesos was the obligation left to us, and we have paid this in full.

We worked hard to accumulate the funds government has today, which is why we will not tolerate wasting it. If our Bosses choose the right leaders, succeeding administrations will be able to surpass what we have done because our administration has greatly reduced the number of problems remaining, giving them a stronger foundation from which to begin.

Why do we say a stronger foundation? Just this past 2013, for the first time in history, the Philippines was upgraded to investment grade status by Moody's, Fitch, and Standard and Poor's—the three major credit ratings agencies in the world. Through their study of our macroeconomic fundamentals and governance, they determined that there was less risk, which led to a vast increase in confidence on the part of investors. Just this May, they upgraded the Philippines yet again. What this means: Because the Philippines is now investment grade, government will be able to borrow funds for programs and projects at lower interest rates, more businesses will be attracted to invest in our country, and Filipinos will be able to feel the benefits of our economic resurgence more quickly.

If anyone were to add up all the investmentsthat came in through the Philippine Economic Zone Authority (PEZA) since its inception in 1995, they would see that 42 percent of total investments in PEZA came in during the four years of our administration. The remaining 58 percent took 15 years for past administrations to accumulate.We are confident that, before we step down from office, we will be able to match or even surpass this amount. To Director General Lilia de Lima: thank you for all you have done and for all that you will do to achieve this success.

Our economy and our country are indeed taking off, and we are already realizing even greater aspirations. For instance, we inherited a seemingly grounded aviation industry: significant safety concerns had been issued on the Philippines by the International Civil Aviation Organization, or ICAO; we were downgraded by the United States Federal Aviation Administration; and the European Union implemented restrictions against our local carriers.

In 2013, ICAO lifted the significant safety concerns it had previously issued for the Philippines. This was followed, in the same year, by the European Union lifting the ban on Philippine Airlines, allowing it to fly once again to Europe—which means that Filipinos will be able to fly directly from Manila to London.

Naturally, Cebu Pacific will soon follow suit, since they have also received the go signal from the EU in 2014. In this year, as well, the United States Federal

Aviation Administration upgraded the Philippines back to Category 1. Because of this upgrade, it is likely that there will also be an increase in routes going to the United States. The increase in flights of our local airlines to the United States and participating countries in the EU is a big help to both tourism and business.

Today, we continue to receive news that, because of all the tourists and businessmen who wish to visit the Philippines, there is actually a shortage of flights to our country. So, all of the upgrades we have received in aviation are indeed good news: The number of flights will rise, thus providing a solution to the problem. And, through the continued cooperation of the CAAP and our local carriers, we will certainly be able to attract more businessmen and tourists in the coming years. This is a win for all those in the tourism sector; this is a win for the Filipino people. Good governance is the source of these upgrades, and we thank Director General William Hotchkiss, the CAAP, and our local carriers for their hard work.

Indeed, the Philippines is in the limelight on the global stage. Just this May, when we successfully hosted the World Economic Forum on East Asia, we showed the world just what we were capable of. And with the APEC Summit the Philippines will be hosting next year, we will be able to inform even more people of our progress, and the opportunities that this has opened up for all. There is no doubt: the Philippines is indeed more open for business.

Apart from fostering an improved busines climate, we are also pursuing better relations between labor and managment.

Consider this: According to the National Concilation and Mediation Board, since 2010, the number of strikes per year has been limited to less than ten. This is the positive result of the Department of Labor and Employment's Single entry Approach, or SEnA, through which filed labor cases go through a 30-day conciliation-mediation period. The good news: out of 115 notices of strike and lockout in 2013, only one pushed through. This is the lowest number of strikes in the history of DOLE.

For these achievements, I extend my gratitude to Secretary Rosalinda Baldoz, the DOLE family, and the labor and management sectors.

Secretary Baldoz and I were joking in around 2012 that there were two strikes, and in 2013 there was just one. I said, "Linda, in 2014, a half-strike won't do. Maybe we can strive for no strikes?"

We are well aware that we need infrastructure in order to sustain the momentum of our economy and to continue creating opportunities in the country. Infrastructure will entice businessmen—it will speed up the transport of goods and services, and will help us ensure that we can go head to head with overseas markets.

This sector has seen massive changes: Our budget for infrastructure has more than doubled from the 200.3 billion pesos of 2011 to 404.3 billion pesos this 2014.

I remind everyone: we did this without adding any new taxes, apart from the Sin Tax Reform, which is focused on health, while we maintained our allowable deficit, and with our debt-to-GDP ratio continually declining. This has had a profound effect, because we have not only increased the infrastructure budget, we have also plugged leaks in the system, which has ensured that the citizenry is getting more value for its money.

Under the leadership of Secretary Babes Singson of the Department of Public Works and Highways (DPWH): Neither kickbacks nor overpricing is condoned. The loopholes in the old system were plugged, the agency's processes were streamlined. A simple example would be the removal of Letters of Intent from the bidding process. In the past, these bred a culture of collusion—knowing who was bidding on the same project only created a space for collusion. Another example: The requisite documents from bidders were trimmed to five, from 20. Processes are faster, and there are now fewer opportunities for the unscrupulous to ask for bribes. This allowed the Department to save 28 billion pesos and allowed them to accelerate the implementation of the next projects.

To Secretary Babes and the DPWH: Again, thank you very much.

It is truly awe-inspiring: In addition to what the DPWH has saved, the roads that they have laid out, fixed, widened, or constructed have amounted to a total of 12,184 kilometers.

When I saw these figures, I thought: How can I visualize 12,000 kilometers?

Think of it this way: This is equivalent to four roads that connect Laoag to Zamboanga City. And this just only accounts for the national roads; that number doesn't include local farm-to-market roads or tourism roads.

Now, regarding the Public-Private Partnership program: From December 2011 to just this June, your government has awarded and signed off on seven PPP projects, with a total value of 62.6 billion pesos. In just our four years on the straight path, we have surpassed the combined six approved solicited PPP projects of the past three administrations.

The difference between then and now is massive. As Secretary Cesar Purisima said: In the past, the Philippines could not entice investors; then, the government had to roll out incentives like commercial development rights, subsidies, and other guarantees for profit just to attract bidders. Now, the situation has reversed. Companies are now in close competition, trying to outdo each other; they are ready and willing to pay for the privilege to build the infrastructure we need. For example, with the Mactan-Cebu International

Airport Passenger Terminal Building, the government has a premium that amounts to more than 14 billion pesos; with the NAIA Expressway Project Phase 2, the government received a premium of 11 billion pesos. Again: Good economics is borne of good governance.

Let us take a look at the TPLEX. Because of this road, the journey from Tarlac to Rosales in Pangasinan has become easier. According to the proponents of the project, the segment of the road that reaches Urdaneta will be completed before the year ends. And by next year, the TPLEX will have extended to the end of Rosario, La Union.

Infrastructure projects that long ago had been promised by other administrations, we have been able to turn into concrete reality. The Aluling Bridge, which was conceived in 1978, is finally open to the public. Metro Manila Skyway Stage 3, part of the Metro Manila Expressway project from the 1970s, was launched this January. Those who traverse Osmeña Highway can attest to how speedily its columns are being constructed. The Ternate-Nasugbu Road, the plans for which started to be laid out in 1994, is now 100% complete.

The Basilan Circumferential Road, which has been under construction since 2000, will soon be completed. These are but a few of the infrastructure projects that we do not intend to pass on as problems to succeeding administrations; instead, our Bosses have already begun to make use of them.

Again, because of good governance, we now have a greater capacity to find solutions to problems that are on the horizon. For example: water. We all know that as our population grows and as our economy continues on its upward trajectory, the country will need a greater water supply in the coming years. According to some studies, there may be a shortage of water in Metro Manila by 2021. We will not wait for a drought: The solutions that experts have studied assiduously, we have already approved—the Kaliwa Dam Project in Quezon, and the repair of the lines of Angat Dam. These solutions are significantly better than sourcing water from underground aquifers, which are more easily penetrated by saltwater. On top of this, if we were to rely solely on aquifers, then we would only hasten the sinking of land—which would contribute to flooding.

Together with the dams for Metro Manila and its outlying cities, we are providing support to those in the provinces. We have also approved the Water District Development Sector Project, under the Local Water Utilities Administration.

You may have already heard of our largest PPP project—the Laguna Lakeshore Expressway Dike. [Applause]—for which bidding will open before the end of 2014. This is a project that will yield numerous benefits. First: flooding in nearby areas will lessen. Today, when water levels of the Laguna Lake reach 12.5 meters, surrounding communities will be flooded. The solution: a dike with a height of more than 15 meters. Second: the water of Laguna Lake will be cleaner. Third: Less traffic. An expressway will be built on top of the dike, which will extend from Los Baños to Taguig. When the C-6 road that will connect to San Jose Del Monte is completed, we will have another route that will allow us to travel through Metro Manila without passing through EDSA.

With the cooperation of the private sector, the only obligations we have in this project are for the right-of-way; and a portion of the reclaimed land will serve as payment for the highest bidder. Because of this,we will get what we need, while spending less in the process.

These are only a few examples of the projects that are in the pipeline, and that will soon bring benefits to our Bosses. Might I add—there are many more: the NEDA Board has likewise approved the Laoag City Bypass Link Road Project; the Cebu Bus Rapid Transit Project; and the LRT Line 1 South Extension and Line 2 East Extension. For those of our countrymen from Palawan: Apart from the projects for the Puerto Princesa Airport, there is also the Busuanga Airport to look forward to. We have likewise given the go signal for the construction of phase one of the modern Clark Green City in Capas, Tarlac, that will certainly serve as a center for commerce and industry, not only of Central Luzon, but also of the entire country. At the end of the day, our vision for Clark Green City is that it becomes even bigger than the Bonifacio Global City. Formerly isolated places will now become areas teeming with opportunity.

Through good governance, we have been regaining the trust of the market, of the world, and of our own people, in government. This is creating a virtuous cycle: Seeing the results of our reform agenda has spurred the active participation of each and every one of our Bosses. Indeed: today the government is not alone in pushing for widespread and meaningful reform. It is true that you are our strength.

This is why, Boss: We thank you for your trust and your solidarity, both of which have become even more significant in the times when we were faced with tragedies that came to us, one after the other.

In September of 2013, lawless elements attacked Zamboanga; our countrymen who had been living peaceful lives there were used as human shields, their homes were burned down. This crisis tested the caliber of our uniformed services. Urban combat is considered the most complex kind of combat; in spite of this, our troops were able to save 195 of the 197 Filipinos caught in the conflict. We salute our countrymen in the uniformed services: Your sacrifice paved way for the victory of the Filipino people.

Following the incident, we gave Secretary Singson the responsibility of overseeing the rehabilitation of damaged infrastructure in Zamboanga. The first priority: to provide shelter to our countrymen who lost their homes to fire. This is exactly what we are doing under the Zamboanga City Roadmap to Recovery and Reconstruction. By this coming August, affected families can begin to move into permanent housing units in Martha Drive Subdivision. We also aim to complete the construction of 7,176 housing units in other areas by June of next year. I must ask for your understanding. There were many problems surrounding the land for resettlement—problems we had to address. On top of this: We also had to make sure that the houses that would be built would be in accordance to the beliefs and culture of the beneficiaries; these will not be ordinary houses. On the other hand, to the 1,661 families that wish to build back or repair their own homes, 30,000 pesos worth of Home Materials Assistance is now being distributed.

We have set aside 3.5 billion pesos for the rehabilitation of infrastructure, the purchasing of lots, the construction of permanent houses, and other types of assistance for Zamboanga. 2.57 billion pesos from this fund has already been released to the NHA and DPWH.

A few weeks after the crisis in Zamboanga, Central Visayas was rocked by an earthquake, which left Bohol the most devastated. In the midst of a calamity, we witnessed just what could be achieved when our people come together to respond to the challenges brought by a disaster. For instance, just one week after the earthquake, electricity was restored in Tagbilaran and in all the municipalities of Bohol.

Now, each of the 25 critical roads and bridges destroyed by the earthquake are passable. 3.583 billion pesos has already been released for the rehabilitation of Bohol and Cebu.

Part of this is the 2.49 billion pesos that the DILG provided to the local government for the reconstruction of markets, civic centers, bridges, water systems, municipal halls, and other government facilities.

Before the end of 2013, Yolanda made landfall. It was the strongest typhoon in history, affecting 1.47million families and 44 out of our 81 provinces. In Eastern Visayas, where the damage was most severe, so many issues required immediate attention.

The immense strength of the storm paralyzed many LGUs that were hit directly. The relief goods we prepositioned were swept away, which is why relief had to come from areas farther away. The delivery of aid was made all the more difficult by the destruction of infrastructure. There was no electricity, roads were impassable, and almost all of the trucks and heavy equipment that our first responders needed had been destroyed in the areas most affected by Yolanda.There was no gasoline, and there was no communication.

It required an enormous amount of solidarity to assist affected families, take care of the wounded and of those who lost loved ones, and make certain that there would be no outbreak of disease, among many other responsibilities. Let us look at the delivery of food as an example: It was not just a matter of buying rice and canned goods. We needed repacking centers, several trucks, and boats that would bring aid to affected provinces. When the relief goods arrived, we had to be sure that the roads to the affected areas were cleared, and that the trucks had enough gas to return home, and load even more of our food packs.

Your government wasted no time in responding. We immediately cleared the airport, which is why, within 24 hours after the storm, three C130s were able to bring in aid. On that same day, we were also able to set up a communications hub to hasten the flow of information. On the second day, the Department of Health's Rapid Health Assessment teams arrived, as well as additional soldiers, policemen, and BFP personnel from other provinces. Likewise, workers from DSWD lead relief operations—in the distribution centers in Eastern Visayas or in repacking centers all around the country.

In a span of two days, the Leyte water district resumed operations; on the third day, the first gas station opened. The main roads were immediately cleared. By the 22nd of November, which was two weeks after the storm, the one millionth food pack was distributed to the victims; we had cleared 35,162 cubic meters of debris from these roads through which the relief will be transported; and 3,426 kilometers of National Roads had already been cleared and were passable. At present, we are repairing the 108.8

kilometers of destroyed roads, bridges, approaches, and landslide prone areas. By Christmas Day of 2013, all municipalities affected by the calamity had been electrified.

We took an emergency room mindset; the state utilized its full strength to stabilize the patient in the soonest possible time. I extend my gratitude to the members of the Cabinet, who led the government response in the affected communities. Secretary Cesar Purisima, along with Secretary Joel Villanueva of the Technical Education and Skills Development Authority, organized the logistics in the repacking center, taking on the role of warehouse operator.

Secretary Greg Domingo of the Department of Trade and Industry became the country's head purchasing agent, while Secretary Linda Baldoz of the Department of Labor and Employment served as a call center operator for all those who wished to help.

I also thank Secretary Jun Abaya of the Department of Transportation and Communications, who dispatched our transportation; Secretary Dinky Soliman, who proved that she was worthy of being the country's chief relief worker; and Secretaries Mar Roxas of the Department of Interior and Local Government and Secretary Volts Gazmin of the Department of National Defense, who were on the disaster frontline, giving marching orders to our uniformed services.

To the members of our Cabinet, thank you.

To our friends and neighbors around the world: Your outpouring of solidarity will never be forgotten by a grateful Filipino people. Again, on their behalf, we thank you.

Perhaps, given the Filipino people's readiness to render assistance to the best of our abilities—a characteristic embodied by our OFWs, peacekeepers, and all our other countrymen abroad—when the world saw that we were in need, they saw fit to come to our aid. Today, we express once more our gratitude to all of you, and to all the Filipinos who have offered their prayers and their support, whether here, or in other parts of the world.

Our work did not end there. We implemented livelihood interventions, to ensure that those of our countrymen who survived the typhoon could recover at the soonest possible time. This July, 221,897 jobs were created after we turned over boats, fishing and farming equipment, seeds, and livestock to our countrymen. This includes those Filipinos to whom we paid salaries for participating in the cash for work program.

Perhaps everyone can agree that Yolanda left in its wake a massive problem. According to international standards, whenever a calamity of this scale takes place, it normally takes a country one year before it transitions from relief to rehabilitation. However, in just a span of eight months, the United Nations declared the Philippines to be in the rehabilitation state. In fact, Mr.

Yuri Afanasiev of the United Nations Development Program said, "We have never seen a recovery happen so quickly. And many of us have been in many different disasters."

It will indeed take a long time for any country to recover and rise from massive calamities. In Haiti, two years after the earthquake, there are still many who live in evacuation centers. For our brothers and sisters in Indonesia, it took eight years before they recovered from the tsunami in Aceh. And even in America, it is said that it took eight years for things to return to normal after the devastation of Hurricane Katrina.

Our work is not done. There are still many houses that need to be constructed; many more of our countrymen need to be assisted in getting back on their own two feet; the work to build back better for all those affected by Yolanda continues.

This is why this July, the LGU Rehabilitation and Recovery Plan for Cebu, Iloilo, Eastern Samar, Leyte, and Tacloban City was submitted to me, and I have signed it.

It passed the scrutiny of our cabinet clusters; according to the holistic post-disaster needs assessment that was conducted, the plan encapsulates the needs of our countrymen. This plan was formulated as a result of the dedication of Secretary Ping Lacson, whom we tasked with focusing on the challenges left by Yolanda.

I am hoping for the cooperation of Congress, because a large sum is necessary in order to help our countrymen make a full recovery.

Let us remember: God proposes, but man disposes. This is likewise the idea behind our efforts for disaster preparedness. We are strengthening the capabilities of our LGUs, who are the frontliners in times of disasters, through a modern and comprehensive forecasting system.

Through the DREAM-LiDAR project under Project NOAH, for instance, we can more efficiently pinpoint areas that are prone to flooding. 19 out of our targeted 20 river systems have already been mapped, to determine which areas immediately suffer from the effects of torrential rain.

Because we can more efficiently determine when and where typhoons will affect us, today, we are able to give our LGUs sufficient warning—and thus give them ample time to prepare, and to evacuate their constituents. If we were to add the efficiency of LGUs to our already-efficient forecasting system, then, without a doubt, countless lives can be saved. In Albay, which recently had to endure the wrath of Typhoon Glenda, there were no recorded casualties attributed to the storm, thanks to the effective leadership of Governor Joey Salceda.

And if a province that is considered a highway for storms can achieve this, is there any doubt that any and all other LGUs can achieve the same?

Let us now talk about security. We are aware of the challenges our country faces, and we also know the high cost of the equipment we need. Today, I am glad to report to you the ongoing modernization of the AFP. We have acquired brand new assets, including 8 Sokol Combat Utility Helicopters, 3 AgustaWestland-109 helicopters, and the first landing craft utility ship built right here in the country: the BRP Tagbanua. 4 refurbished UH-1 helicopters and 2 navy cutters have also arrived.This past May, we also inaugurated the Naval Forces West's state-of-the-art Command Center in Palawan.

We expect the rest to be delivered in 2017. We are also targeting the acquisition of an additional 8 Bell combat utility helicopters, 2 anti-submarine helicopters, 10 more AgustaWestland-109 helicopters, 2 light-lift aircraft, 3 medium-lift aircrafts, radar systems, all of which are brand new. These, along with other new equipment, will boost the capacity of our Armed Forces.

Meanwhile, we are expecting the delivery of 17 additional refurbished UH-1 helicopters by September of this year.

The M4 assault rifles we bought for our soldiers have likewise arrived. In the next few months, the total number of rifles that will be in the hands of our soldiers: 50,629 units. On top of this, through a correct and transparent procurement process and the honest management of funds, we were able to save more than 1.2 billion pesos. [Applause] which we will use to purchase even more rifles.

I must emphasize: all these rifles are brand new and of good quality from a veteran manufacturer. Was it not true that, before, our funds were depleted in the purchase of Kevlar Helmets that were not even according to specification? Instead of buying them from the U.S., these helmets were purchased from another country. There has already been a conviction over this matter. The investigation of a judge who was allegedly involved, which was ordered by the Supreme Court, has been concluded as well, and we are awaiting their verdict.

We are continuing our pursuit of enemies of the state and lawless elements for the crimes they have committed. For example: We apprehended the Chairman and Secretary General of the NPA this March. Normality and order are now returning to the 31 provinces previously troubled by the NPA.

The image of our police has changed. Proof of this are the 30 policemen, led by Inspector Charity Galvez, who repelled an estimated 250 NPA members who stormed their precinct in 2011.

Just last March, four rookie policewomen bravely exchanged fire with the Martilyo Gang in the

Mall of Asia. It is indeed fortunate that we have already reached a 1:1 police-to-pistol ratio, which is why these rookie policewomen were issued brand new guns. Before, the needs of our police force went ignored; today, the state is taking care of them, and indeed, they are matching this support with efficient and upright service.

Let us listen to our brave policewomen:

Testimonials of Juliet Macababbad, Marcelina Bantiyag, Maricel Rueco, and Delia Langpawen—policewomen who arrested members of the Martilyo Gang

PO1 Juliet Macababbad: We heard glass breaking, and my partner and I immediately went on alert.

PO1 Marcelina Bantiyag: The first thing that came to my mind was to draw my gun, because I knew that they would be ready to shoot at us—we were in uniform.
PO1 Maricel Rueco: My partner, PO1 Bantiyag said, "I'll cover you. Call our Police Community Precinct."

PO1 Marcelina Bantiyag: We caught one of the gang members.

PO1 Delia Langpawen: It was only our fourth day on the job, at that post. And then that happened.

PO1 Juliet Macababbad: Every police officer needs a gun. Thankfully, they issued us a Glock 17 Generation 4.

PO1 Marcelina Bantiyag: Guns are essential to us. If something bad happens when you're on patrol, you're confident that you can engage.

PO1 Juliet Macababbad: It feels good when you know you're able to help your fellow citizens. Whatever a man can do, a woman can do just as well.

PO1 Delia Langpawen: Even if we were nervous, because it was our first encounter, we were thinking of the safety of all the people that were there. [Applause]

This past June, we had a succession of high-profile killings. We have already arrested some of thoseinvolved in the murders of Mayor Ernesto Balolong and businessman Richard King, and are currently following a strong lead in the murder case of race car driver Ferdinand Pastor. Rest assured: we are seeking justice for all, and not just for a few. This is why, on top of the arrests we have already made, we continue to gather evidence against other suspects. We will hold to account all those who have committed wrongdoing.

We are further strengthening ways to ensure the security of our citizens. Beginning June 16 of this year, we implemented Operation Lambat in the National Capital Region. After tripling the number of checkpoints and conducting various operations, we were able to confiscate 862 vehicles and 29 firearms. We have served 587 warrants of arrest, which have resulted in the arrest of 410 suspects. We also reinstated Oplan

Katok, to ensure that the licensing of guns is limited to responsible owners. Our policemen knocked on 28,714 doors for this operation.

Before we implemented Operation Lambat, from January to the second week of June, the rate of murder and homicide cases in Metro Manila reached up to 31 cases a week. During the five weeks of Operation Lambat, murder and homicide cases decreased to only 22 cases per week. This is a 29 percent decrease, equivalent to nine murders prevented per week. And this is only in Metro Manila. If we are able to pass pension reform, which would enable us to gather even more funds to continue our planned purchases of equipment, then Secretary Mar Roxas will certainly be able to expand Operation Lambat, and thus make the whole country more secure.

These equipment purchases were supposed to be funded by DAP, but since they were not obligated before the Supreme Court made its decision, we now have to look for other sources of funds.

Indeed, trust is the foundation of good governance: the trust that all those who were affected—or who will be affected—by typhoons will be cared for; the trust that, after each day of work, you will be able to return home safely to your families; the trust that your leaders will not take advantage of you; the trust that government will always be by your side, especially when you find yourselves at a disadvantage. The trust that those who abuse their power will be held accountable, and the trust that the institutions and processes that were once abused and used to steal from the nation's coffers will be reformed. The trust that, if you do what is right, you, in turn, will receive what you deserve. The restoration of your trust in government: this is the meaning of reform.

Let me give you an example: Customs, which had been sorely testing our patience these past years. It became clear to us that the solution to the problem this agency represented was a reset button. Thus, we created a new agency to look into the processes at Customs, with an eye towards making them more efficient. We appointed a new commissioner, five new deputy commissioners, as well as 40 trustworthy individuals to implement our reforms. We ensured that employees were recalled to their original positions—we put a stop to guards who acted like cashiers, or warehousemen who acted as examiners.

Many have made sacrifices just so we can fix Customs. Among them are officials from other departments and government agencies, who we asked to transfer to Customs because we were certain of their integrity. Who would have said yes to taking on these seemingly insurmountable challenges, and without the guarantee of success? Some passed on promotions. Some expressed fears of being targeted by syndicates, in retaliation for the reforms. But, ultimately, they heeded our call to serve. It is only right that I take this opportunity to personally thank these officials, under the leadership of Commissioner Sunny Sevilla.

We are proving that, with righteousness and with solidarity, we can clean up an institution that has, for the longest time, been besmirched by corruption. Recent good news is testament to this—from January to April of 2014, Customs' cash collections increased by 22 percent, compared to the same period last year. Their collections total in the first four months of the year: 117 billion pesos.

All I can say to those who continue with their selfish, illegal practices: I already know that you are impervious to both fear and shame. I will leave you to your conscience—if you feel any remorse for your fellowmen who have become addicted to the illegal drugs you have helped to smuggle in, or for the farmers who are being deprived of fair profit from doing honest work. As far as I am concerned: After we have gathered enough evidence against you, the Bilibid Prison is your next destination.

If we are talking about reforms that have already begun to give rise to sweeping progress, we have to touch on recent developments in agrarian reform.

We know—and the law is very clear about this—that we must first determine which tracts of land can be distributed and which cannot. The trouble is, we were provided with data too insufficient to be of any help in this regard. The Cadastral Survey—which was supposed to accurately delineate the territory, and, thus, the land holdings, of every town, city, and province of the Philippines—was launched way back in 1913.

Another problem is that the previous administration had distributed land that was easy enough to distribute—like government-owned land, or land already settled between the farmers and the deed-holders. We were left with land that came with too many complications—that only spawned endless debates and legal disputes.

The complicated situation in ARMM proved to be another challenge. The land in ARMM is estimated to be at 1.5 million hectares, but the recorded number of hectares we found when we came into office was at 2.9 million, thanks to overlapping claims. ARMM Governor Mujiv Hataman must be wondering—as he has sometimes asked me: How does land multiply like that?

I have no intention of passing on these problems to my successor, which will cause even greater complications and a standstill in agrarian reform.

In 2015, after 102 years, the Cadastral Survey will finally be completed.

This year, we will once again submit to Congress a bill extending the filing of Notices of Coverage, which could not be completed precisely because of these problems that we first needed to solve.

We are hopeful that, the moment we file that bill, Congress will pass it in the soonest possible time.

If we are to speak of trust, then we cannot forget about the Bangsamoro. After a lengthy period of conflict and derailed negotiations, we were able to put trust back to the table. Proof of this: This past March, the Comprehensive Agreement on the Bangsamoro was signed.

But this is only the beginning of the path toward widespread progress in Mindanao. Nobody can deny that the ARMM has been left behind in terms of development. We want to give equal opportunities to all Filipinos; this is why there is a need for a boost-up, so that our countrymen in the margins can catch up. For example, in the budget we are submitting for 2015, 5.17 billion pesos of the overall budget for DPWH has been allocated for infrastructure in ARMM.

We are currently forging the proposal for the Bangsamoro Basic Law. We ask for the Congress' understanding regarding this. It is important to scrutinize each provision we lay down. To the best of our ability, we aim to advance a bill that is fair, just, and acceptable to all.

If we are able to legislate the Bangsamoro Basic Law before the end of the year and conduct the necessary plebiscite, we will be able to give the Bangsamoro Transition Authority one and a half years to show positive change. Should this be delayed, however, the period for proving that it was right to choose the path of peace will naturally be shortened.

We have achieved a lot through trust—and we have no intention of breaking this trust. Your current government keeps its word. I will no longer list each of the promises we have fulfilled by treading the straight path; if I do that, we might be accused of bragging. But of course, it would not be right for us to avoid mentioning anything, because our critics are always waiting for an opportunity to say that we have done nothing. Join me, then, in recounting some of the examples of these promises we have fulfilled: Jobs and opportunities that continue to be created for so many Filipinos. In truth, from April 2013 to April 2014, around 1.65 million jobs were created. [Applause]

The inherited backlog in books, chairs, and classrooms: erased; while we are working to fulfill the new needs brought about by the implementation of K to 12. The 1:1 police-to-pistol ratio has already reached. The modernization of the Armed Forces, currently ongoing. A just and lasting peace in Mindanao, already advancing. Growth of the economy, progressing continuously.

Truly, our ambitions are now being fulfilled one by one: universal healthcare, classrooms, jobs, harbors, roads, airports, security, peace. In addition to the national integrity we have restored is the world's recognition of a new Philippines. The nation's coffers, which come from the sweat of our citizens, are being spent only for their benefit.

Let us again listen to one of our Bosses:

Testimonial of Gina Lastrado, relocated member of an informal-settler family

I am Gina Lastrado, 47 years old. I used to live at Isla 1 Barangay 180, in Maricaban, Pasay City. I was a businesswoman back in Pasay. Currently, I still make a living selling goods; it's a job that demands hard work.

We were relocated here because the place we used to live was tagged a "danger zone"—most of the houses were right beside a river.

When typhoon Ondoy [international name, Ketsana] hit, it was terrible. You wouldn't have believed that we would survive.

If you compare our lives back in Pasay to our lives now—here, it rains, it storms, but you can sleep through a night. There's no lying awake, worrying about the coming flood—not like where we used to live. Which is why I told my friends, those who stayed behind, to relocate, too. Here: There's no fear, there's no flood.

When we got here, they gave us groceries, they gave us the key to the house, then they brought us to our house. And the eighteen thousand pesos they gave us, that helped us start a new life. This gave us back our dignity, all of us who

were living in the squatters' area back in Pasay. Our lives are much better here. You can say that this is really our home now.

Now: the problems we inherited, we have solved. The problems that are here today, we are solving. And the problems that are still on the horizon, we are preparing for. I believe; with your continued trust, we can solve all of these.

Let us turn to the energy situation. We are doing everything in our power to ensure that the growing energy demand in our country is met. In spite of this, there have been some unforeseen events, that may lead to problems in the next year. For instance, we need to make up for the shortages caused by the scheduled maintenance outages of old plants, the sudden halting of plant operations due to breakdowns, and delays in the progress of new plants.

Let us not forget that the coming El Niño season also threatens to affect the capacities of our hydro power plants, and to raise energy demand even further. If our use of electric fans and air conditioners in our own homes will increase due to the warm temperature, then imagine the spike in the usage of businesses and whole industries. And it is not as if we can just go to the store and ask to buy a 600 megawatt generator, to be installed the following day.

We want to be completely ready so that we can avoid paralysis if the worst-case scenario arises. The goal: to have planned solutions for problems that will not arise until next year. This is precisely why I have tasked Secretary Icot Petilla of the DOE to coordinate with the Joint Congressional Power Commission, the Energy Regulatory Commission, members of industry, and, most importantly, the consumers, in order to increase our capacity to respond to this problem.

I am also aware that many of our Bosses are affected by the staggering increase in rice prices. It seems that the reports are true: that some greedy rice hoarders are stockpiling their supplies in order to sell them when prices eventually rise, making an unjust profit in the process.

We will not let this pass. Perhaps they think they are being clever, but the government's plan of action will prove the opposite. Our immediate solution: import more rice, supply it to the markets, reduce the prices and keep them at a reasonable level, and ultimately drive those who took advantage of the Filipino people into financial ruin.

Last November, we imported 500,000 metric tons of rice to supplement decreased supply due to the typhoons that battered our country, and all of this had arrived by March of this year. This February, the NFA Council approved the importation of an additional 800,000 metric tons, in fulfillment of our buffer stocking requirement, and as of this July, 360,750 of this amount had arrived. This July as well, we approved the immediate importation of 500,000 metric tons of rice through open bidding. The NFA also has the standby authority to import an additional 500,000 metric tons to prepare for the effects of calamities on harvests and rice prices.

When the additional rice we have imported arrives in the country, hoarders will be forced to sell the rice that they have stockpiled in their warehouses. To these hoarders: If a showdown is what you want, by all means, take on the government. Just remember: it only takes six months before the stock you have hoarded in your warehouses begins to rot. When we flood the market with this imported rice, you will surely go bust. You are acting against the Filipino people, while we are acting for the interest of each Filipino. Let us see who will prevail.

Apart from investigating those who have allegedly hoarded NFA rice, we are also probing all those in concerned agencies who may have conspired with these hoarders. Employees suspected of wrongdoing are already under scrutiny, so that we may file charges, and eventually, imprison those who must be held to account.

While we are in pursuit of those abusive few, we have also continued to implement projects to uplift Filipinos in the sector of agriculture. We are ensuring that rice farming remains a viable and attractive livelihood. After all, we know that our farmers are advancing in age, which is why it will help our pursuit of food security to encourage the youth to enter this kind of work.

We are providing our farmers with modern equipment to ensure the efficiency of planting and harvest. From 2011 to May 2014, we have already turned over 4,628 units of production machinery, 11,362 units of post-production machinery, and 105 rice mills to a number of farmers' associations. This has allowed us to lessen waste in what our farmers are able to harvest. On top of this: we are also enhancing irrigation systems, constructing farm-to-market roads, and implementing training programs to ensure that they make the maximum profit.

Now, let us turn to the budget. The Executive Branch proposes projects, which are approved by Congress. However, we have had to suspend a number of projects to make certain that we remain in accordance with the Supreme Court's decision on the Disbursement Acceleration Program, or DAP. I know that those of you in this hall are one with me in believing that we must not deprive our countrymen of benefits, and that these should reach them in the soonest possible time.

This is why: We are proposing the passage of a supplemental budget for 2014, so that the implementation of our programs and projects need not be compromised.

Together with this, we are calling on the cooperation of Congress for the passage of a Joint Resolution that will bring clarity to the definitions and ideas still being debated upon, and to the other issues that only you in the legislature—as the authors of our laws—can shed light on.

On the first working day after the SONA, we will submit to Congress the proposed 2.606 trillion peso National Budget of 2015. As always, this budget was created together with our countrymen, using strategies that will ensure that funds are only allocated to projects and programs that will truly benefit the public. We are counting on the cooperation of our lawmakers to strengthen our Budget, as the primary instrument in creating opportunities for the Filipino people.

Let us now listen to one of the beneficiaries of our Alternative Learning System, A program of the Department of Education.

Testimonial of Maria Cecilla Fruelda—Aeta tribal leader, Alternative Learning System learner, and college student

I am Maria Cecilla Fruelda. I heard from my friends who also came from Zambales, and who are now living here in Rosario, that there are good jobs to be found in Puting Kahoy. That's why we moved here.

Our first priority as tribespeople has always been to look for food, rather than to invest time in our education. But

education is very important to me. Passing the Alternative Learning System (ALS) was the first step in realizing my dream of becoming a teacher.

I think that young Aetas in my community would have much better lives if only they could study.

If I hadn't gotten into ALS, I wouldn't have learned about our rights as indigenous peoples. We wouldn't be able to fight for our ancestral land. Right now, thank God, the National Commission on Indigenous Peoples is processing land titles to be awarded to us.

Once I graduate with a degree in Education, I want to teach in our community. I want to share with the Aeta community everything I've learned and more.

The ALS has been such a great help. My being a student of Teodoro M. Luansing College of Rosario has helped bring more attention to our community. A lot of people have offered to help. I see our community's children following in my footsteps. A lot of them are in school now.

Fellow citizens, It is her story—and the stories of many other beneficiaries like her—that is drowned out by the din of the orchestra of negativism in the news. These noisy individuals willfully close off their minds and choose to live in their own world and reality. As the transformation of society becomes even more apparent, these people are acting just how we expect them to: their attacks on us are becoming more frequent, more venomous, and more intense. As the benefits of reform become clearer, it becomes more and more difficult for them to succeed in fooling the people, which is why they are sowing doubt and uncertainty. They have become desperate.

Why are they so angry? Let us examine their motivations. For those who turned public service into a business: if we are able to fix our systems, they lose the opportunity to subvert these systems for their own gain. It is only natural that they oppose us. On the other hand, for those who have no other goal than to overthrow government: They can only recruit members when agreat number of people are suffering and losing faith in the system. This is why, with a reformed system that has ended the people's suffering, the number of potential recruits has dwindled, which explains why their group is getting smaller and smaller. It is only natural that they oppose us. The noisiest and loudest of those who oppose us are not in favor of the transformation of our country, precisely because they manipulated and benefited from the old and broken systems.

It was as if we were citizens who had been long trapped in an island with only one store. Since there were no other choices, the store owners abused their advantage, raising prices whenever they wanted. The task you gave me was to steer our ship of state to another island, where there were more stores, more choices, better lives, and more opportunities. Of course, those running the solitary store in the island did not want us to set sail, because they will run out of people to abuse. They would do everything in their power to prevent us from reaching other shores. They would say that it is no different there, and that nothing would change. They would detain us at the port, punch holes in our ship, and conspire to steer us astray.

The truth is that I am not the one these people oppose, but the entire Filipino people who are now reaping the benefits of the straight path. They oppose the farmers in Iloilo, who have hoped for efficient irrigation systems for more than fifty years, and today are witnessing the construction of the Jalaur Multi-purpose River Project.

They oppose the countless students who no longer have to study in overcrowded classrooms. They oppose the Filipinos who have found jobs because of training received from TESDA; the Filipinos who have been safely evacuated before typhoons strike because PAGASA is now more efficient; they oppose the informal settlers who have been removed from danger because of housing resettlement programs; they oppose the poor who can receive treatment from public hospitals free of charge; they oppose the soldiers who, because their equipment has been modernized, can now protect our nation with greater confidence; they oppose the Moros and indigenous peoples who, today, see a just and lasting peace on the horizon. My Bosses, they are against you.

In fact, their attacks began even before we came into office. We have grown used to being greeted by negative commentators for breakfast, personal attacks for lunch, insults for dinner, and intrigue for a midnight snack.

And even now that I am President, those opposed to change have not changed their ways. To be frank, I do not think that they will stop even when I have stepped down from public office.

I recall an old woman who I spoke to during the campaign. She told me: "Noy, you must take care of yourself. You will be up against many people." Her warning proved to be true. But my resolve is unshakeable when it comes to facing them down, because I know: they are but a few, and there are so many of us.

Those of us who are ready to fulfill our part in achieving positive transformation are, without doubt, stronger. We will triumph because we are in the right.

We dared to dream, we began pursuing those dreams, we worked hard, we gained the momentum, and today, the Filipino people are moving even faster along the straight path to lasting and inclusive growth.

Our fatigue and sacrifices will be all the more worthwhile if you are able to continue what we started together.

It is you who will face a fork in the road; it is you who will decide if change will continue. Let us remember: This my fifth SONA; only one remains. In 2016, you will be choosing new leaders of our country. What I can tell you is this: if you wish continue and even accelerate the transformation of society, there can only be one basis for choosing my successor: Who will, without a shred of doubt, continue the transformation we are achieving?

You are our bosses, you are our strength, you are bringing about change –and so it is you, too, who will continue the task. It is entirely up to you how history will remember this era. They may recall it as the very peak of our triumphs, as a promising start that went to waste. But it would be infinitely better if they remember our achievements as the beginning of a long journey towards the fulfillment of even more ambitious hopes.

When some groups appealed to me to run for President, they told me that they did not expect to solve all the country's problems in a span of six years. They simply asked me to begin the change. You saw where we came from, and you are seeing how we have far surpassed the aspirations with which we began.

We are forging a system of fairness; where, as long as you follow the rules, you can get to where you want to go; where true competition leads to opportunity and widespread progress; where each and every person can take control of their own destinies.

A society where the least fortunate are cared for is within reach; where each person recognizes his responsibilities to his fellowmen; where there is an unceasing, untiring, ever-active participation in collectively increasing the prosperity of society.

The future we desire is on the horizon: one where justice reigns supreme, and where no one will be left behind.

These are the results of reform. This is what we have fought for, and this is what we will continue fighting for: not the prevalence of the old ways, but a new system that will benefit all.

To my Bosses: You gave me an opportunity to lead our efforts to transform society. If I had said "no" when you asked me to take on this challenge, then I could just as well have said that I would help prolong your suffering. I cannot do that in good conscience. If I had turned my back on the opportunity, then I might as well have turned my back on my father and mother, and all the sacrifices they made for all of us; that will not happen. On our journey along the straight path, you have always chosen what is right and just; you have been true to your promise, and I have been true to all of you.

The transformation we are experiencing now, we can make permanent with the guidance of God. As long as your faith remains strong—as long as we continue serving as each other's strength—we will continue proving that "the Filipino is worth dying for," "the Filipino is worth living for," and if I might add: "The Filipino is worth fighting for."

The Vice President knows this—we were together in 1987. There was a coup de etat, and I was ambushed. Everything after that I consider my second life.

It's hard not to think about these things, considering the people we've been going up against. Will there be a day when I go onstage, for work, and—will someone manage to plant a bomb? Will the dark schemes of those who want to bring us back to the wrong way of doing things finally succeed?

When that day comes, and my second life comes to an end, will I be able to say things will be ok? I will tell you this, straight in eye: after everything we've achieved, I can say that I am content.

I am content because I am sure that when I'm gone, many will take my place and continue what we have started.

Maybe this is what I'm meant to do: to start this.

There are people like Cardinal Chito Tagle, Ka Eduardo Manalo, Brother Eddie Villanueva, Father Catalino Arevalo, and Father Jett Villarin, Bishop Jonel Milan, Sister Agnes Guillen, and Mae Salvatierra. These are individuals from the religious sector, who will continue what we've started.

There is Aris Alip of CARD, who will do his part through microfinance. There is an Alice Murphy and her urban poor associates who will truly continue to take care of our informal settlers.

There are our soldiers and police officers, who try every day to do what is right—just like our new Chief of Staff, our Service Commanders, our soldiers in the Light Reaction Battalion, and the JSOG.

There are, of course, my fellow politicians. Is there any doubt that Senate President Franklin Drilon and Speaker Belmonte will lead us along the right path?

It has also been my privilege to work with and interact with a certain governor, Alfredo Maranon of Negros Occidental:

He is not a party mate, but I think I am part of his fan club because of his good governance in Negros.

There are up and coming young politicians. Or at least they're younger than I am—I don't want to seem too much like an old politico by referring to my colleagues as young.

These are the likes of Mayor Jed Mabilog and Mayor Len Alonte.

There is also those in the cultural sector—such as Noel Cabangon and Ogie Alcasid-—who are not self-centered.

Every night, before I go to bed, I am thankful that I was able to get through another day. Just as it was said when we were kids, "finished or not finished, pass your paper." It seems to me, you have felt the true extent of the change that is every Filipino's right to aspire to. It will be up to you to carry this forward.

To my Bosses: You are behind the transformation we are enjoying. You are the key to continuing all the positive changes we have achieved. I fully believe that, whether I am here or not, the Filipino is headed towards the rightful destination.

And so, I will leave it here. Good afternoon to all of you. Thank you very much.

My Book List - Contact:
job_elizes@yahoo.com -   tatay@usa.com

My website - http://tinyurl.com/mj76ccq

Writings 1 Book, 2012 + + 1. Obit, *Bambi Harper* **+ + 2. Speech, UP, 2003,** *Butch Jimenez* **+ + 3. Speech, Silliman U, 2006,** *Butch Jimenez* **+ + 4. The Mission Moment,** *Dr. Phil Stack* **+ + 5. Subanon Spirits of Rice & Land -** *Noel Cornel Alegre* **+ + 6. I Look Out The Window -** *Atty. Toto Causing* **+ + 7. Ride On A Bus, Poem,** *Melanie Ferrer, et al* **+ + 8. Why Am I Doing This,** *Susie Barbieri* **+ 9. How To Court A Philippine Lady,** *Rodel Ramos, et al* **+ + 10. Story of Bacna Surgical Mission,** *Sylvia Salvador* **+ + 11. Catch That Story,** *Tatay Jobo Elizes*

Writings 2 Book, 2012 + + 1. There Is Hope For The Philippines, *Grace Padaca* **+ + 2. Pointers On Employment Abroad,** *Melanie Aquino* **+ + 3. Without KNCHS: (Love story),** *Atty. Toto Causing* **+ + 4. 422 Years Ago,** *Rodel Rodis* **+ +5. Filipino American History Month,** *Rodel Rodis* **+ + 6. A Need For Reflection, Gloom,** *Cesar Torres* **+ + 7. Did Ninoy Die For Nothing,** *Joey Concepcion* **+ + 8. Criteria - American Institute of Philanthropy, Charity Guidelines (Feature)** **+ +9. Coming Revolution In The Ballot,** *Cesar Lumba* **+ + 10. 2009, A Retrospective,** *Cesar Lumba* **+ + 11. Strangers In Our Own Country,** *Casiano Mayor Jr.* **+ + 12. The Gypsy Soul,** *Casiano Mayor Jr.* **+ + 13. An End To Cheating,** *Sonny Coloma* **+ + 14. Toward Culture of Giving, Not Having,** *Sonny Coloma* **+ + 15. 100 Reasons to be Proud as Pinoys,***Anonymous*

Writings 3A Book, 2012 + +
1. EPIC25, Emerging Philippines Investors Coalition, *Norman Madrid* **+ + 2. Management Ability As An Issue,** *Dr. Rene B. Azurin* **+ + 3. Do We Really Want To Give Our Politicos More Power,** *Dr. Rene B. Azurin* **+ + 4. Will 2010 Fulfill Filipinos High Hopes For Better Life – Metamorphosis,** *Ernie D. Delfin* **+ + 5. Comelec Is The Root Of All Evils,** *Toto Causing* **+ + 6. Some Advantages of Federalism and Parliamentary Government For The Philippines,** *Dr. Jose Abueva* **+ + 7. Sometimes A Great Nation,** *Mar-Vic Cagurangan* **+ + 8. Great Conspiracy,** *Mar-Vic Cagurangan* **+ + 9. Of Speech & Life's Riddles,** *Casiano Mayor* **+ + 10. Bad Start To The Year,** *Rod Garcia* **+ + 11. A Dinner out,** *Rod Garcia* **+ + 12. One More Time,** *Roy Gaane* **+ + 13. Strange Noises –** *Tatay Jobo Elizes* **+ +**

Writings 3B Book, 2012 + +
1. The Reeds and Beams of Sunset in Paite and Balangaging in

Zambales, *Ceres Busa* + + 2. Memories of your Past, *Ceres Busa* + + 3. Blowout in the Barrio, *Ceres Busa* + + 4. Dream on Sari-sari Store Keeper, *Ceres Busa* + + 5. O Naraniag O Bulan, *Ceres Busa,* + + 6. Candelaria, O Candelaria, *Ceres Busa* + + 7. Four P's ... Pastillas, Pilipig, Patupat at Panan, *Ceres Busa* + + 8. On Being Filipino American, *John Reyes* + + 9. The Monterey Peninsula, *John Reyes* + + 10. The Salaza Fiesta, *John Reyes* + + 11. Salawikain: Filipino Proverbs, *John Reyes* + + 12. Musikero (The Musician), *John Reyes* + + 13. Did You Know (1), *Bert Guiang* + + 14. Did You Know (2), *Bert Guiang* + + 15. Did You Know (3), *Bert Guiang* + + 16. Did You Know (4), *Bert Guiang* + + 17. Did You Know (5), *Bert Guiang* + + 18. Sharing Trivia, *Bert Guiang* + +

Writings 4A Book, 2012 + +
1.   The State of Our Nation and Democracy In 2010: Building 'The Good Society" We Want, *Dr. Jose V. Abueva* + + 2. Assessing the Expanded Role of AFP in Nation Building, *Col. Dencio (Dennis) Acop, Ret,* + + 3. Assessing RP's Security Strategies, Alternative Views, *Col. Dencio (Dennis) Acop, Ret.* + 4. The Way We Were, *Fred Natividad* + + 5. Veterans of Ipo Dam, A Fiction, *Fred Natividad* + + 6. A Plea, *Miguel Reyes Reynaldo* + + 7. International Youth Bowling, My Impressions, *Marjorie Ann Elizes Reyes* + +

Writings 4B Book, 2012 + +
1. Mi Ultimo Adios (My Last Farewell), *Dr. Jose P. Rizal* + + 2. Aling Pagibig Sa Tinubuang Bayan, *Gat. Andres Bonifacio* + + 3. Rekonsilasyun Dula (Reunion in Heaven), *A Play, Irineo P. Goce (KaPule2 or Leonidas P. Agbayani)* + + 4. Forgery of Rizal Retraction, *Irineo P. Goce (KaPule2 or Leonidas P. Agbayani)* + + 5. Maikling Kasaysayan Ng Malas Na Bayang Pilipinas, *Ireneo P. Goce (KaPule2 or Leonidas P. Agbayani)*

Writings 5 Book - "Best Hopes" 2010, About President P-Noy + + I. The Challenge of a Hundred Days: Believing that Filipinos can, *Tony Meloto* + + II. The 2006 Ramon Magsaysay Award for Community Service, *for Tony Meloto* + + III. Open Letter to Noynoy, *F. Sionil Jose* + + IV. A History of Pain, *Juan L. Mercado* + + V. An Open Letter to Noynoy, *From OFWS* + + VI. Pursuit of Good Governance Advocacies, *Marcelo Tecson* + + VII. A Fervent Prayer for Peace, *Cesar Torres* + + VIII. A History of Betrayal, *Perry Diaz* + + IX. Corona's Thorny Crown, *Perry Diaz* + + X. Dawn of a New Era, *Perry Diaz* + + XI. Of Mice, Boys and Men, *Philip S. Chua, MD* + + XII. A Hopeful Tomorrow - A Balikbayan Insight, *Philip S. Chua, MD* + + XIII. Global Filipinos: A Sleeping Giant, *Philip S. Chua, MD* + + XIV. Heart to Heart - Winds of Change, *Philip S. Chua, MD* + + XV. Growing Old is a Privilege, *Philip S. Chua, MD* + + XVI. Our Cruelty to Mother Earth, *Philip S. Chua, MD* + + XVII. Advice to Grads: "Never Choose Your Heroes Lightly", *Ernie Delfin* + + XVIII. Gawad Kalinga, A Progressive Movement, *Ernie Delfin* + + XIX. Why a Man Must Save and Invest, *Ernie Delfin* + + XX. Beautiful San Francisco, Pinoy Heaven, *Ted Laguatan* + + XXI. The next President and PAMUSA, *Frank Wenceslao* + + XXII. Philippne Budget Deficit, *Frank Wenceslao* + + XXIII. Money Laundering: US Tools vs. Corruption, *Frank Wenceslao* + + XXIV. Amid the Fighting, Clan Rules Maguindanao, *Jaileen F. Jimeno* + +XXV. Why I Publish Writings, *Tatay Jobo Elizes*

Writings 6 Book, 2010 + + I. SONA, State Of Nation Address, English, *Pres. Benigno Aquino III* + + II. SONA, State of Nation Address, Pilipino, *Pres. Benigno Aquino III* + + III. First 100 Days Speech, Pilipino, *Pres. Benigno Aquino III* + + IV. Finally, Another Ramon Magsaysay In The Making, *Bert Guiang.* + + V. A Covenant With Our President, *Tony Meloto* + + VI. From A Grateful Heart, A Thank You Letter, *Tony Meloto* + + VII. The Scent of Hope For The Global Filipino, *Tony Meloto* + + VIII. Fleshing Out The Broad Strokes, *Felicito (Tong) C. Payumo* + + IX. In Search Of Leaders (Part1), *Felicito (Tong) C. Payumo* + + X. In Search of Leaders (Part 2), *Felicito (Tong) C. Payumo* + + XI. A Conspiracy of Dunces, *Cesar Lumba* + + XII. Only Science Can Solve Poverty, *Flor Lacanilao* + + XIII. Education Reform Amid Scarcity, *Flor Lacanilao* + + XIV. Highblood: Obituaries/Reasons, *Flor Lacanilao* + + XV. How Money Works, *Edmund Lao* + XVI. State of Economy & Society, 2002, *Juan Dela Cruz (Txtmania)* + + XVII. Global Filipinos, *Juan Dela Cruz (Txtmania)* + + XVIII. Understanding Poverty, *Juan Dla Cruz (Txtmania)* + + XIX. Kuyakuy, *Dr. Ramon Marquez* + + XX. Cambodian Octopus, *Joey Jamito* + + XXI. Inspite Of Herself, I Still Love The Philippines, *Joey Jamito* + + XXII. Love Has Wings, *Percy Campoamor Cruz* + + XXIII. Walk For Kris, *Rod Garcia* + + XXIV. Coldblooded, But Alive, *Rod Garcia* + + XXV. It Takes A Village, *Rod Garcia* + + XXVI. Beauty Contest, *Rod Garcia* + + XXVII. Eight Points In Enlightening The Elites, *Orion Perez Dumdum* + + XXVIII. Case Against "Cellphone Revolution", *Sarah Raymundo*

Writings 7 Book, 2010 - My Vintage Pics (Biographical) Tatay Jobo Elizes

Writings 8 Book, 2010 + + I. The Church and the State: In Search of Common Ground, *Gel Santos Relos* + +II. President Aquino: "Walang Kaibigan, Walang Kamag-anak", *Gel Santos Relos* + + III. What Makes Us "Pinoy", *Gel Santos Relos* + + IV. Minsan May Isang Puta (2007), *Mike Portes* + + V. Build Our Dream, *Jose Ma. Montelibano* + +VI. Hope In Europe, *Tony Meloto* + + VII. Wealth in Canada, *Tony Meloto* + + VIII. Parenthood: A Sacred Covenant, *Philip S. Chua* + + IX. Are We, Humans, Really Civilize? (Or, are we for the birds.), *Philip S. Chua* + + X. Save Our Nation, *Philip S. Chua* + + XI. A Time To Pause, *Philip S. Chua* + + XII. The Gawad Kalinga Virus, *Philip S. Chua* + + XIII. A Marching Order For P-Noy, *Philip S. Chua* + + XIV. "Bayan Ko" Bonds, *Philip S. Chua* + + XV. P-Noy's First 99 Days, *Philip S. Chua* + + XVI. The Practice of Quackery in the Phils, *Cesar D. Candari* + + XVII. Remember When? A Brief History of Old and Recent Past, *Cesar Candari* + + XVIII. The Philippines Before and What Now?, *Cesar D. Candari* + + XIX. The Traffic Problems are Beyond "Wang-Wang", *Cesar D. Candari* + + XX. Behind The Gold, *Eliseo Serina* + + XXI. May Angal? (Any Complaint?), *Greg B. Macabenta* + + XXII. Pagbalik-Tanaw Sa Kapatirang Masoneriya Sa Pilipina, *Irineo P. Goce* + +XXIII. Mysteries & Riddles Behind RP's Corridors Of Power, *Irineo P. Goce* + + XXIV. Wika - Diwa Ng Lahi, O, Ang Tore ni Babel Sa Pilipinas, *Irineo*

Heart to Heart, Are We Getting Enough Sleep, *Philip S. Chua* + + 21. Heart to Heart, Obesity: A Killer, *Philip S. Chua* + + 22. Are we the disappearing breed of professionals in this country?, *Cesar D. Candari* + + 23. If You Dream It, Do It Retirement, *Cesar D. Candari* + + 24. Only In America, Human Interest Story, *Anonymous*

Writings 11 Book, August, 2011 + + 1. SONA In English and Filipino, *Pres. Benigno Aquino III (P-Noy)* + + 2. Telltale Signs: SONA and the Dogfight Over Spratlys,   *Rodel Rodis* + + 3. Why China will not bring the Spratlys issue to the United Nations,   *Ted Laguatan* + + 4. Random Thoughts, On Website Demise and On Disunity, *Tatay Jobo Elizes* + + 5. Can Local Private Sector Help Reverse Philippine's Migration Addiction?,*Jeremiah M. Opiniano* + + 6. What Fuels the Passion of Filipinos to Pursue Studies and Work in UK?, *Ofw Journalism Consortium* + + 7. Our Life in the Philippines, *Bob & Carol Hammerslag* + + 8. Reality Check: the Philippines – A Tropical Paradise for the Retiree?, *by Bob & Carol Hammerslag* + + 9. Filipinos Dominate Cruise Ships, *Roger P. Olivares* + + 10. Vargas: Hero, Villain, Tragic Figure?, *Roger P. Olivares* + + 11. Is it Hell to go Back Home?, *Roger P. Olivares* + + 12. The Filipino, now a commodity!, *Roger P. Olivares* + + 13. How US Can Create Jobs, *Rob Ceralvo* + + 14. Modus Operandi - Common Crimes (In Metro Manila, Philippines), *Anonymous* + + 15. Poem, Kabuhayang Bansa At Wika, *Irineo P. Goce (aka KaPule 2 and Leonidas Agbayani)* + + 16. Random Sayings & Advices, *Anonymous*

Writings 12 Book, April 2012 + + 1. Twenty Excuses Filipinos Use, *Orion Perez Dumdum* + + 2. One By One, The Petals Drop, *Julia C. Lagoc* + + 3. Religion & the Scientist, *Honorio M. Cruz, MD* + + 4. The Tales of the Aswang & Bangungot, *Honorio M. Cruz, MD* + + 5. Sex & Politics, *Honrio M. Cruz, MD* + + 6. Autopsy, *Ben Gonzales, MD* + + 7. Geekmocracy, *Mar-Vic Cagurangan* + + 8. Flights: Voice from the Future that Lives in the Past, *Mar-Vic Cagurangan* + + 9. Kaya Natin! Sanctuary, *Marisa Lerias* + + 10. The Days of Courage, *Gerry Partido* + + 11. Earth Day and the Tragedy of a Famous River, *Cesar D. Candari, MD, FCAP Emeritus* + + 12. Few Filipino-American NonprofitsGetting Political, *Erwin De Leon* + + 13. Filipino-American Political Invisibility And Community Organizations, *Erwin De Leon* I+ + 14. I'm 32 and I am still a Virgin, *Jovelyn Bayubay Revilla* + + 15. Hiding Ill-Gotten Wealth, *Jobo Elizes*

Writings 13 Book, July 2012 + +
1. From "Criminal" to "Doctor" in Criminal Justice, *Raymundo E. Narag* + + 2. The Essence of Giving, *MLMunoz* + + 3. My Prescription for Spiritual Life, *Sonja Barbara dL Munoz* + + 4. Anak Ng Prosti, *Pamela Joy Agtoto* + + 5. Ang Kapangyarihan ng Kanyang Pag-ibig, *Percival Campoamor Cruz* + + 6. Ang Tato ni Apo Pule, *Percival Campoamor Cruz* + + 7. Rapture, *Percival Campoamor Cruz* + + 8. Ang Taong Walang Anino, *Percival Campoamor Cruz* + + 9. Gender Formula – Boy or Girl, *Tatay Jobo Elizes* + + 10. The Single, *Jhackie Eslit Bayobay* + + 11. Why I Am Angry, *Jhackie Eslit Bayobay*, 12. Rules of Living, *Jhackie Eslit Bayobay* + + 13. Being Alone, *Jhackie Eslit Bayobay* + + 14. Love and Hurt, *Jhackie Eslit Bayobay* + + 15. My First Heart Aches, *Jhackie Eslit*

Bayobay + + 16. Why the Philippines Need Sex Education, *Reygel Saplad Perales* + +

Timely Writings 14, 2013 + +
1The Giant Sucking Sound and the Rise of Employnomics, *Cesar Fernando Lumba* + + 2. UP, College of Bus. Admin. and Cesar E.A. Virata, *Eugenio Pulmano* + + 3. The Missing Element in Education Reform, *Late Sec. Jesse Robredo* + + 4. China: Some Observations from My Recent Trip, *Antonio Nievera* + + 5. Don't invest in stocks if you don't have these, *Alvin T. Tabanag* + + 6. Creating Your Own Financial Plan, *Alvin T. Tabanag* + + 7. Anti-Gay Hate Crimes on the Rise in New York City: A Call to the Community, *Kevin L. Nadal, Ph.D.* + + 8. Native Colonialism & Subjugation, *Anonymous (TJ Friend)* + + 9. The Way We Were - Fond Look at a Hometown, *Fred Natividad & Bing Castillo* + + 10. Obituary: Common Sense, *Anonymous* + + 11. Be The Best Ever, *Anonymous* + + 12. Remembering Capt. Rene N. Jarque, *Ellen Tordesillas* + + 13. Why I Left the Military, *Late Capt. Rene N. Jarque* + + 14. Soldiers In Elections: From Pawns to Knights, *Late Capt. Rene N. Jarque* + + 15. Reforming The Armed Forces - *Late Capt. Rene N. Jarque* + +

Timeless Writngs-15, May, 2014 + +
1 - Protecting the Nation's Marine Wealth in the West Philippine Sea, *By Supreme Court Justice Antonio T. Carpio* + + 2 – Are Filipinos United Against China's Invasion of Ayungin Shoal, *By Rodel Rodis* + + 3 – Telltale Signs: Why Are There So Many Nurses in the US? *By Rodel Rodis* + + 4 – Telltale signs: Philippines – A Jewish Refugee from the Holocaust, *By Rodel Rodis* + + 5 - Telltale Signs: OFW Remittances Promote Mendicant Culture, *By Rodel Rodis* + + 6 – Adding Insult To Injury: UP College Named After Marcos' Prime Minbister, *By Ted Laguatan* + + 7 - Aquino To Nation: "This Is Your SONA." *By President Benigno Aquino III* + + 8 – Why We Are Poor: A Purpose for the Middle Class, *By F. Sionil Jose* + + 9 - Secrets of a Romantic Man, *By Dr. Phil Stack* + + 10 - Totoong Buhay Sa Canada, *By Racz Kelly* + + 11 - Small Steps to Building a Nation, *By Bert Armada* + + 12 - The Rising of a Nation. *By bert Armada* + +

Timeless Writings Book – 16 , July 2014 + +
1. The Martyrs of Camarines Norte, *by the heirs* + + 2. The Self-Perpetuating Elite of the Philippines, *by Rodel Rodis* + + 3. Isang Open Letter Tungkol sa Trapiko, *by Ragulane* + + 4. Truest Yet Rendered Death Ode of Rizal by *Robert M. Bernardo, 2014* + + 5. Aquino SONA 2014: PNoy's 5th SONA Full Transcript (English version), *by Pres. Benigno Aquino III* .

Solo Authored Books: + + +

Book A, **Turning Points,** *Job Elizes Sr,1968 (Reissue 2009)* + + +
Book B, **Be Considerate For Once,** *Tatay Jobo Elizes (Jr), 2013*
Book C, **Piglets Unlimited - Wealth,** *Tatay Jobo Elizes, 2009* + + +
Book D, **Out of the Misty Sea We Must,** *Cesar Lumba, 2010* + + +
Book E, **Fulfilled** - *Gonzales Reynaldo, Editor, 2010* + + +

Dook F -   **Reflections** - *Bert Guiang, 2010* + + +
Book G,   **Writings 7 - My Vintage Pics,** *Tatay Jobo Elizes, 2010* +
Book H,   **May Bagwis Ang Pag-ibig,** *Percival C. Cruz* + + +
Book I,   **Letters To Matrimony,** *Irineo P. Goce, Ka Pule2, 2011* +
Book J,   **Songs I Wish You Knew,** *Soledad R. Juan, 2011* + + +

Book K,   **Make My Day,** *Larry Henares Jr., 1993, Re-issue 2011* +
Book L,   **Our Guerrero Family,** *Tatay Jobo Elizes, 2010* + + +
Book M,   **Handy Jokes,** *Tatay J. Elizes, 2011* +
Book N,   **FaveArt 1,** *Tatay Jobo Elizes, 2011* + +
Book O,   **Beyond idle thoughts,** *MLMunoz, Sept,2011* + + +

Book P, **Cracks In The Armor,** *Mariano Ngan, Oct 2011* + + +
Book Q, **FaveArt 2,** *Tatay Jobo Elizes, 2011* + +
Book R, **Balitang Kutsero,** *Perry Diaz, Jan 2012* + + +
Book S, **FaveArt3,** *Tatay Jobo, 2011* + + +
Book T, **FaveArt4** *,2012, Tatay Jobo* + + +

Book U, **Stack Family Journals,** *Phil & Fe Stack, 2012* + + +
Book V, **Emily, An Adoption Journey,** *Romerl Elizes, 2012* + + +
Book W, **Hermes Alegre Art Gallery,** *TJ & Hermes, 2012* + + +
Book X, **Masaya Din, Malungkot Din,** *Jovelyn B. Revilla, 2012*
Book Y, **Tiis, Sipag At Tiyaga,** *Raquel Delfin Padilla, 2012* + + +

Book Z, **Until I Meet You,** *Jhackie Eslit Bayobay, 2012* + + +
Book AA, **Buhay At Pag-ibig,** *Argel Lucero Tamayo, 2012* + + +
Book AB, **Hail to the Second Best,** *Dr. Philip Stack, 2012* + + +
Book AC, **Life Bus,** *Mommy Joyce Pineda-Faulmino, 2012* + + +
Book AD, **My Candid Musings,** *Monette Dioquino Calugay, 2012* +

Book AE, **Tickets to Life,** *Maria Lourdes Jesalva, 2012* + + +
Book AF, **The Dove Files,** *Mike Portes, 2012* + + +
Book AG, **Nursing Vignettes,** *Jocelyn Cerrudo Sese, 2012* +
Book AH, **Poor Ba Us,** *R.A. Gubalane, 2012* + + +
Book AI, **Summer Idyll,** *Avelina Gil, 2012* + +

Book AJ, **Legacy (Pamana),** *Rachel Astrero, 2012* + +
Book AK, **Narratives Old & New,** *Avelina J. Gil, 2013* + +
Book AL, **Buhay Saudi,** *Adele J. Esic, 2013* + +
Book AM, **Buhay Ofw Atbp,** *Jessica Napat, 2013* + +
Book AN, **Mga Tula Ng Buhay,** *Angelita C. Esguerra, 2013* +

Book AO, **Not by Bread Alone,** *Judge Lily V. Magtolis, 2013* +
Book AP, **Jokes Collection-2,** *Tatay Jobo Elizes, 2013* + + +
Book AR, *My Writings Sometimes, Tatay Jobo Elizes, 2013*
Book AS, **Sa 'Yo Na Ako,** *Shayne A. Martinez, 2013*
Book AT, **My Kin's Family Trees,** *Tatay Jobo Elizes, 2013*

Book AU, **Rizal Family Tree & Others,** *Tatay Jobo Elizes, 2013*
Book AV, **Make My Day-2, Nice & Nasty,** *L. Henares, 2013 (1993)*
Book AW, **Make My Day-3, Cecilia, Love,** *L.Henares, 2013 (1993)*
Book AX, **Handy Lyrics-1,** *Tatay Jobo Elizes, 2013*

Book AY, **Ang Biblos,** *Rev. Dr. Eugenio Guerrero,* ***2014 (1929)***

Book AZ, **Make My Day-4,** *Sweet & Sour, L. Henares,* ***2014 (1993)***
Book BA, **Life's Journey, True Stories,** *Dr. Phil Stack,* ***2014***
Book BB, **Gerry Gil Writings-1,** *Danny Gil,* ***2014***
Book BC, **Mr. President,** *Hermie Rotea,* ***2014***
Book BD, **Nostalgic Pics** *1, Tatay Jobo Elizes,* ***2014***

Book BE, **MakeMyDay-5, Saints & Sinners,** *Henares,* ***2014 (1993)***
Book BF, **MakeMyDay-6, Villains & Heroes,** *Henares,* ***2014 (1993)***
Book BG, **Nostalgic Pics 2 (ElizesClan),** *TatayJE,* ***2014***
Book BH, **MakeMyDay-7, Tough & Tender,** *Henares,* ***2014(1993)***
Book BI, **MakeMyDay-8, Light & Shadow,** *Henares,* ***2014(1993)***

Book BJ, **MakeMyDay-9, Give & Take,** *Henares,* ***2014(1993)***
Book BK, **MakeMyDay-10, ToBeOrNotToBe,** *Henares,* ***2014(1993)***
Book BL, **Emily Forever In Love,** *Emily Espanol Derry,* ***2013***
Book BM, **The Sinatra Songbook,** *Henares,* ***2014***
Book BN, **The Gaborro Reader,** *Allen Gaborro,* ***2010***

Book BO, Ramon H. Lopez *- Art Gallery, **2014***
Book BP, Philippines Via Old Pics-1, *Tatay Jobo,* ***2014***
Book BQ, Ronna Manansala *- Art Gallery,* ***2014***
Book BR, Philippines Via Old Pics-2, *Tatay Jobo,* ***2014***
Book BS, Being Good-A Medley Of Love, *Dr. Phil Stack,* ***2014***

Book BT, Lifestream Fisherman, A Fil.Odyssey, *Paul Dalde, Jul2014*

Please buy online or give as gift in paperback or kindle edition. All authors and titles are easy to search, trace or find online. Thanks. Self-Publisher, Tatay Jobo Elizes

Philippine Sea Scene

Phillipine Beach Scene

Philippine Coconut Trees at beach

Philippines Mount Kanlaon in Negros

Philippines Mount Pinatubo in Zambales

Philippine River Scene

Philippine Riceland Scene

Philippines Ferryboat scene

Philippines rural road scene

Philippines Beach Scene

www.ingramcontent.com/pod-product-compliance
Lightning Source LLC
Chambersburg PA
CBHW050404290526
45786CB00003B/1125